The Reliable Expert Witness

The Reliable Expert Witness

Mark Tottenham

Published by
Clarus Press Ltd,
Griffith Campus,
South Circular Road,
Dublin 8.
www.claruspress.ie

Typeset by
Gough Typesetting Services,
Dublin

Printed by
SprintPrint
Dublin

ISBN
978-1-911611-33-2

A catalogue record for this book is available from the British Library

To Fionnuala

Contents

Chapter 3
Enforcement of Experts' Duties

Chapter 4
Accepting Instructions

Contents

Contents

.

About the Author

Mark Tottenham is a barrister and mediator. He was the lead author of *A Guide to Expert Witness Evidence* (Bloomsbury Professional 2019), the leading Irish legal textbook on expert evidence, which won the Dublin Solicitors' Bar Association's Practical Law Book of the Year award, 2020.

He was the founding editor of *Decisis.ie*, an online publisher of law reports, and *Decisis Law Ireland (DLI)*, a monthly law–reporting journal. He has written for *The Irish Times*, *Irish Independent*, *Laffoy's Irish Conveyancing Precedents*, *Conveyancing and Property Law Journal*, *Medico-legal Journal of Ireland*, and is the editor of the *Irish Tax Reports*. He has lectured at the Kings Inns, the Law Society of Ireland, and the school of architecture at the Dublin Institute of Technology (now Technical University, Dublin).

He is a graduate of history from Trinity College Dublin. He formerly worked as a genealogist, and for Hodder Headline publishers in London.

Preface:
The Nature of Expertise

Everybody needs experts. There are many topics on which we need to consult people who know more than us to teach us, to inform us, and to advise us on the important decisions in our lives.

From early childhood, these experts are our parents, who teach us to tie our shoelaces and ride a bicycle. We then rely on school teachers to teach us to read, write, add and subtract. The older we get, the more specialised the knowledge we are taught, whether we are learning how to plaster a wall, to review a set of financial accounts, or to carry out a medical operation.

Experts also impart information. In most families and groups of friends, there are some who know more about how to fix a bicycle or put up a shelf, some who know more about how to cook a meal, and some who know more about the best films to watch. Much of the information we receive from experts is in books, newspapers, television or online videos.

Some expert information must be kept confidential, and can be highly valued. The rules on insider trading are designed to prevent people with specialist knowledge from giving it to people who will used this information to buy or sell shares or bonds.

The advice we receive from experts is most critical when we are making decisions. For small decisions, we can often rely the advice of family or friends. For bigger decisions, we rely on professionals.

The very term 'professional' encompasses an ambivalence. These people are paid to advise, yet their very professionalism can incorporate a conflict of interest. If professionals advise clients to take one course of action, they may earn significantly more money than if they advise them to take another.

There are also different levels of expertise. For ordinary medical complaints, we attend general medical practitioners. The more serious or complicated the complaint, the more specialised the medical expert we require. To carry out building work on a period residence requires more specialised knowledge than is required to complete an extension on a modern house.

Many of us fear that we are easy prey to professionals. When we consult plumbers about a small leak, we worry that they will take a look at it, shake their heads sadly, audibly inhale, and tell us we need the entire system replaced at immense cost. A visit to a mechanic about a noise in the engine, or a trip to the dentist about a mild toothache makes us anxious about similarly expensive results. Turning to another person in the same field for a second opinion is not always the answer. Consulting another expert can be expensive, and may only serve to confuse us. We need to trust the professionals who advise us, but feel that we cannot be sure that they are trustworthy.

'All professions are conspiracies against the laity,' says Sir Patrick Cullen in *A Doctor's Dilemma* by George Bernard Shaw. Although Shaw put the words in the mouth of one of his characters, the preface to the play is a lengthy attack on the medical profession, suggesting that doctors made their business from trading on public fears, and that they were resistant to scientific breakthroughs until public demand forced them to change. Among Shaw's conclusions was:

> Treat every death as a possible and under our present system a probable murder, by making it the subject of a reasonably conducted inquest; and execute the doctor, if necessary, as a doctor, by striking him off the register.

The professions have always been an easy target for satirists. On the album *An Evening Wasted with Tom Lehrer*, Lehrer invents the character of Doctor Samuel Gall (inventor of the gall bladder), and says: 'He soon became a specialist, specialising in diseases of the rich. He was therefore able to retire at an early age.'

At a public level, experts are often derided. In 1950, the British Prime Minister Harold Macmillan was wary about the Schuman Plan, which ultimately gave rise to the European Union. One of his concerns was about the technocratic nature of the plan:

> In the reaction against democratic weakness men have sought safety in the technocrats. There is nothing new in this. It is as old as Plato. Frankly, it is not attractive to our British point of view. We have not overthrown the divine right of kings to fall down for the divine right of experts. This is not a purely British point of view. It is shared by all those who are truly attached to democracy and parliamentary institutions.[1]

As recently as 2009, it was suggested that undue deference was given to experts in the US by the Obama administration. In an article by Wilfred M McClay entitled 'What Do Experts Know?', in *National Affairs* (Fall, 2009) the author took the view that the US was becoming a 'technocracy'. McClay said that the role of experts was to advise, but not to decide:

> They cannot be allowed to speak ex cathedra merely on account of the letters after their names, or the sheepskins on their walls, or the professional associations to which they belong.

He said that if experts were not properly accountable to the American people, it would be 'a betrayal of the very idea of a democratic republic.'

The idea of governmental deference to experts seems very dated now. In the US and the UK, the pendulum very decidedly swung away from technocracy in the years after the economic collapse of 2009. Sometimes it has seemed that the uninformed views of the person on the street were to be given equal footing with the most experienced specialists.

---

[1]   "Anglo-French Split Widens over the Schuman Plan", *The Guardian*, 16 August 1950, page 8.

In 2016, most public experts advised that the UK should not vote to leave the European Union, suggesting it would lead to serious economic damage. Michael Gove, then justice secretary and a supporter of 'Brexit', railed against the 'elitism' of specialist organisations, saying:

> I think the people of this country have had enough of experts from organisations with acronyms saying they know what is best and getting it consistently wrong.

The victory for the 'leave' side in that referendum was portrayed as a victory for the ordinary people who were 'taking back control' of their country from the professional classes.

A similar prejudice against professionals was evident in the US in the same year, when the successful Republican candidate tore up the rule book in almost every sense. As recounted by Michael Lewis in *The Fifth Risk*, each government department had been required by law to prepare expert briefings for the incoming administration, to help them prepare during the transition period. The briefings remained unread by the time the new administration took over, and they appeared to have no interest in learning from the experience of their predecessors.

The new administration seemed to take pleasure not only in appointing people who were manifestly unqualified for their new positions, but also those who had clear conflicts of interest. If the appointees had wanted to act in a professional manner, many of them should have declined the offer of a job simply on the grounds that they were not suitable.

If Michael Lewis's book is to be believed, the consequences of some of this neglect of expertise could be catastrophic. To take one frightening example, in Hanford, Washington State, there are 56 million gallons of nuclear waste – radioactive sludge – buried under a disused nuclear production complex. If this is not managed properly, it will seep into the Columbia River, which serves a number of cities. The proper management would require between $2 billion and $3 billion funding per year for several decades. In June 2019, the President of the United States announced that, to save money, the clean-up was being downgraded. It would be interesting to see the expert advice he relied upon in making that decision.

The worldwide COVID-19 pandemic has demonstrated a clear difference between countries in their respect of health experts. Countries like Japan and South Korea, with recent experience of SARS, took clear, early and decisive action and experienced a small number of infections. While most European countries took relatively early action, Sweden took a notably different path, thanks to a state epidemiologist who advised a course of action that allowed schools, shops and restaurants to remain open, apparently expecting 'herd immunity' to develop. The rate of infections and deaths was notably higher than most other European countries. The US and UK, meanwhile, took less decisive action, and have seen far higher infection and death rates. Both countries have been seen to ignore expert advice, and to pay a higher price.

Every country during the pandemic has had to choose between health experts, who have generally warned about the dangers of allowing economic activity to continue or resume, and economic experts, who have warned about the dangers of not allowing it. Only with the benefit of hindsight will we see who has handled the crisis better.

Reliance on experts is not without risk. Experts can and often do contradict each other. A particular decision may require advice from experts in a number of fields, some of which may conflict. To make a good decision requires the decision maker to be intelligent, open-minded and inquisitive and – where necessary – to ask probing questions of the advice received.

Professionals from many fields may be retained as expert witnesses, and may expect to be challenged in a manner that is probably not common in their day-to-day life. Ordinarily when members of the public deal with plumbers, dentists or mechanics, they do not cross-examine them about their training or their qualifications. They generally do not ask them to provide excerpts from text books to justify their advice. They do not ask how much they stand to gain if a particular decision is taken. Many professionals, if asked these questions by their clients, would be insulted.

In an adversarial judicial system, such questions are standard. Experts can be asked any questions relevant to the issue at hand. Professionals who are eminent in their field may think it impertinent for younger lawyers to ask such questions, but they are obliged to answer them. In this way, ill-prepared experts can be publicly exposed in a way that they would not expect in their ordinary professional life. It is hoped that this small volume will help professional witnesses to teach, inform and advise the courts in an authoritative and reliable manner.

Further reading:

Expert: Understanding the Path to Mastery by Roger Kneebone (Penguin, 2020)

The Philosophy of Expertise by Selinger and Crease (eds)(Columbia University Press, 2006)

Acknowledgements

The idea for this book came from a number of sources. Primarily, I found that when giving training to professionals in how to prepare court reports, they often did not identify with the term 'expert witness'. It was necessary to explain that when the duties of experts were outlined, these generally applied to all professionals who were retained to give evidence.

At the same time, even a cursory review of the case law on expert evidence shows that many professionals have not understood–or chosen not to understand–the requirements of the court, sometimes in quite basic ways.

Different parts of this book have arisen from lectures I have given, or been asked to give, or from conversations with attendees or colleagues. At the time the Covid-19 pandemic led to the initial 'lockdown' in Ireland, in March 2020, I was scheduled to give a number of lectures that had to be postponed. Nonetheless, some of the preparation proved useful in the writing of this book.

I would therefore like to thank the following people and organisations: Noeleen Skelly and Sarah Flynn of CMG Training; Colm Scott Byrne and Eimear Brown of the Kings Inns Medical Law diploma course; La Touche Training; The Chartered Institute of Arbitrators (Irish Branch); The Construction Bar Association; Kerida Naidoo; Yvonne McNamara; Barry Doherty; Deirdre Ní Fhloinn; and John T Garrett, consulting engineer.

I would also like to thank my co-authors and publishers on *A Guide to Expert Witness Evidence* (Bloomsbury Professional, 2019), which is, to date, the only Irish legal textbook on the area. While the book you are holding is a useful guide for professionals, anybody who needs to know the Irish law in the area should obtain a copy of the other volume. My thanks to Emma Jane Prendergast, Ciaran Joyce, Hugh Madden, and all of the staff at Bloomsbury Professional in Dublin.

Individual chapters have been reviewed by friends and colleagues, to whom I owe a great debt of gratitude, most notably: Ronan Rose Roberts, architect; Stephen Mooney, consulting engineer; Dr Simon Mills; and Fionnuala Croker.

I am particularly grateful to Michael Lillis for his encouragement in including his letter about the late Robert Daly in the conclusion to this book. By an odd coincidence, when I was working as a genealogist, nearly 20 years ago, I played a very small part in the research for his book *The Lives of Eliza Lynch*, which he co-wrote with the late Professor Ronan Fanning. So it is serendipitous that his letter provided a useful conclusion to this work.

David McCartney of Clarus Press has been a very enthusiastic publisher, and I would like to thank him for his 'can-do' attitude, as well as the work carried out by the copyeditor, typesetter, proofreader, printer and binder. Having worked in publishing myself, I know how much goes on behind the scenes, although the technology has changed a lot since my days.

Over the years, I have been particularly fortunate to have the support of many other friends and colleagues. It is dangerous to single out anybody, for fear that an exclusion might offend, but I would particularly like to mention: Tig Mays; Arran Henderson; Nick West; Celeste Golden; Valerie Lawlor; Garry O'Sullivan; Keeva Doherty; Frances McLoughlin; Sarah Ryder; and Vincent Walshe. A particular mention should be made of Dr Simon Mills, with whom I shared an office for many years, who is indirectly responsible for my writing this book, and who has been a very useful sounding board on this book and many other issues.

My parents, Richard and Elizabeth Tottenham have been unfailingly supportive of me throughout my life, education and career, and I cannot thank them enough. I would also like to thank my brother,

Philip Tottenham, his partner, Lou Mensah, and my niece Eva, the wider Tottenham family, as well as my parents-in-law, Colm Croker and Nora Ní Ghréacháin, and the rest of the Croker family, and all of my other relatives.

My children, Rosa and Hugh are a source of constant pleasure, and I have had the opportunity to spend much more time with them this year, thanks to the lockdowns. We have been fortunate to live in a place where this led us to spend more time outdoors, swimming and cycling–even if home schooling was something of a secondary concern while both their parents attempted to maintain their careers.

And finally, I could not have started this work, let alone finished it, without the constant love and support of Fionnuala Croker. I am very fortunate to be married to her, and it is to her that I dedicate this book.

A Note on the Law and Legal Principles

This is not a legal textbook. This is a handbook or guide for professionals who are called upon to write reports or to give expert evidence for courts or other hearings.

Readers will note, however, that the book includes many quotations selected from court judgments in several countries. It is important to note that, in most cases, these are expressions of legal principle rather than hard-and-fast rules of law.

Rules of law are distinct to the countries in which the court operates. Legal principles are more universal, but the courts' attempts to define them can evolve over time.

Most countries in the English-speaking world, and many others that were formerly colonised by Britain, have a 'common law' system. This system allows judges to derive rules where no formal rules exist. In other words, where a particular issue is not covered by legislation, or where the legislation is ambiguous, the court can make its own rule. Once that 'judge-made' rule is established, it is normally binding on other courts of equal and inferior jurisdiction in that country, until overturned or amended by a superior court. This is called a system of 'precedent' or, in Latin, *stare decisis*.

When making such rules, the courts often look outside their own country for precedent. Whereas the US courts tend to look to other US precedents, the countries of the Commonwealth, and Ireland, are more open to looking at the case law of other countries.

The issues of the admissibility of expert evidence and the duties of expert witnesses were not extensively discussed in case law prior to the early 1990s. Since then the number of professional and expert witnesses used in litigation has greatly increased. The result is that the courts have been more aware of certain dangers inherent in the use of expert witnesses. Some shocking miscarriages of justice have arisen from questionable testimony by expert witnesses, a few of which are discussed in this book.

As stated above, legal principles are more universal, but may be refined over time and applied to cases before the courts. To take a curious example of how the common law adopts legal principle, in 2016 an obsolete rule of US Federal law was adopted into Scottish law by the UK Supreme Court.

This occurred because, in the US, the rules on admissibility of evidence are set out in a code called the *Federal Rules of Evidence*. The leading federal case in the US on the admissibility of expert evidence is the 1993 case of *Daubert v Merrell Dow Pharmaceuticals*.[2] The court in *Daubert* cited Rule 702 of the *Federal Rules of Evidence*, which used to read as follows:

> If scientific, technical or other specialized knowledge will assist the trier of fact to understand the evidence or to determine a fact in issue, a witness qualified as an expert by knowledge, skill, experience, training, or education, may testify thereto in the form of an opinion or otherwise.

Rule 702 was cited in *Daubert* as the rule that applied to the admissibility of such evidence. (This was in preference to an earlier 1923 test, set out by another federal court in *Frye v United States*[3]).

In 2016, the UK Supreme Court decided a case on the admissibility of expert evidence entitled *Kennedy v Cordia (Services) LLP*.[4] This was an appeal from the courts of Scotland, where the law is generally different from the remainder of the UK. (In fact, in Scottish law, the term 'skilled witness' is generally used in preference to 'expert witness'.)

---

[2]   509 US 579 (1993).

[3]   293F 1013 (DC Cir 1923).

[4]   [2016] UKSC 6 (10 February 2016).

Nonetheless, the UK Supreme Court took a broad and international view of the question of admissibility of expert evidence, including consideration of authorities from England, South Africa, Australia and the US. It stated that Rule 702, as cited in *Daubert*, was 'consistent with the approach of Scots law in relation to skilled [expert] evidence of fact'. It went on to say:

> The advantage of the formula in this rule is that it avoids an over-rigid interpretation of necessity, where a skilled [expert] witness is put forward to present relevant factual evidence in an efficient manner rather than to give an opinion explaining the factual evidence of others. If skilled [expert] evidence of fact would be likely to assist the efficient determination of the case, the judge should admit it.

What the UK Supreme Court did not mention in the judgment – perhaps because it was not discussed in legal submissions – was that Rule 702 had been amended twice since *Daubert*, in both 2000 and 2011. By the time *Kennedy v Cordia* was decided, the rule read as follows:

> A witness who is qualified as an expert by knowledge, skill, experience, training, or education may testify in the form of an opinion or otherwise if:
> (a) the expert's scientific, technical, or other specialized knowledge will help the trier of fact to understand the evidence or to determine a fact in issue;
> (b) the testimony is based on sufficient facts or data;
> (c) the testimony is the product of reliable principles and methods; and
> (d) the expert has reliably applied the principles and methods to the facts of the case.

So, on its face, the UK Supreme Court adopted the pre-2000 US rule into Scottish law, rather than the rule that was in place in 2016. Although they did not say that the obsolete rule was the law in Scotland, they said that it was 'consistent with' the law in Scotland. Any Scottish court seeking to determine an issue of the admissibility of expert evidence would have to follow the authority, including Rule 702 as cited (and not as amended).

In a broader sense, however, the UK Supreme Court was not simply determining an issue of Scottish law. By adopting authorities from the US, Australia and South Africa, it was reviewing not only the law, but the legal principles underlying the admissibility of expert evidence.

The decision in *Kennedy v Cordia* may only technically be binding in Scottish law, but, as a considered decision of the UK Supreme Court it may be treated as effectively binding in the other constituent parts of the UK. It has been cited as such in the courts of England and Wales[5] and Northern Ireland.[6]

Furthermore, *Kennedy v Cordia* has been cited with approval in other common law jurisdictions, including Canada,[7] Australia[8] and Ireland.[9] These courts rely on the decision as a useful review and approval of certain principles concerning the admissibility of expert evidence.

The principle in Rule 702, as cited in *Kennedy v Cordia*, was not overturned by the later amendments to the *Federal Rules of Evidence*. The amendments simply sought to improve upon it in light of US case law, including *Daubert* itself. The UK Supreme Court has adopted the unamended rule as a useful statement of principle, which has now been considered with approval in many other jurisdictions.

Statements of principle are often expressed by the courts as Latin maxims, such as *de minimis non curat lex* ('the law does not concern itself with trifles'), because they often sound pithy, timeless and authoritative. But they can be drawn from other sources, such as the lyrics of Bob Dylan songs. In 1981, the Court of Appeals of California also addressed the question of admissibility of expert evidence, in the case of *Jorgensen v Beach 'n' Bay Realty, Inc*. This is what they had to say:

---

5   *Blackpool Borough Council v Volkerfitzpatrick Ltd* [2020] EWHC 387 (TCC) (25 February 2020).

6   *Graham v Domzala* [2016] NIQB 79 (8 July 2016).

7   *R. v Allingham*, 2018 CanLII 47477 (NL PC).

8   *Gooley v NSW Rural Assistance Authority* [2018] NSWSC 593 (4 May 2018).

9   *C.D.G. v J.B.* [2018] IECA 323 (24 October 2018).

The correct rule on the necessity of expert testimony has been summarized by Bob Dylan: 'You don't need a weatherman to know which way the wind blows.'[10] The California courts, although in harmony, express the rule somewhat less colorfully and hold expert testimony is not required where a question is 'resolvable by common knowledge.'[11]

Questions of admissibility of expert testimony are matters for the legal team, so expert witnesses will not normally need to be familiar with Rule 702, or Bob Dylan's summation. This book does not seek to set down the legal rules on expert evidence as they apply in any one country. The rules will vary from country to country, and are likely to change over time. It does, however, seek to assist professionals to understand, in principle, what is sought from them by courts, arbitrations and other tribunals when they are asked to act as expert witnesses. In doing so, it quotes extensively from the more readable (or, at any rate, less unreadable) parts of judgments of many countries.

Readers who are seeking guidance as to the rules as they apply to their own jurisdiction should consult the legal team that instructed them. In the unlikely event they come into conflict with their own client or legal team, they may need to consult their professional bodies or insurers, or (in exceptional cases) retain their own lawyers. But this book should help professional witnesses to understand how they should approach their tasks.

Note: Nothing in this book should be construed as legal advice.

---

[10] *Subterranean Homesick Blues* (1965).
[11] *Jorgensen v Beach 'n' Bay Realty, Inc.* (Court of Appeals of California, Work J, 2 November 1981) (125 Cal. App. 3d 156).

A Note on 'Common Law' and 'Civil Law' Systems

Most countries in the English-speaking world adopt a system known as the 'common law'. Most non-English speaking countries have a system known as 'civil law'.

Civil law systems have legal rules that are codified, with roots in the Napoleonic code, and – before that – in Roman law. In practice, the courts in civil law countries tend to be inquisitorial, meaning that the judge takes the lead in investigating the facts of the particular case. The legislative code takes primacy, but the courts do look to precedent (i.e. decisions that went before) under doctrine known as *jurisprudence constante* (meaning 'stable jurisprudence').

Common law systems are not based on a governing code but deal with cases as they are presented, relying on a system of precedent knows as *stare decisis* (meaning, essentially, 'that which has been decided'). While legislation takes precedence over *stare decisis*, and is applied by the courts when hearing cases, there are underlying legal principles that the courts have regard to in making their decisions, as discussed in the previous note. Because many of these have their origins in Roman law they have often been expressed as Latin maxims, such as *caveat emptor* ("let the buyer beware") or *semper necessitas probandi incumbi ei qui agit* ("the burden of proof always lies with him who alleges"). In practice, common law courts are adversarial, rather than inquisitorial. This means that the court considers the facts as put before it by the rival parties, and does not normally have an independent investigative role.

Some countries and states, such as Scotland, have hybrid common and civil law systems, unlike the rest of the UK, which is common law. In Canada, Quebec has a civil law system, but the rest of the country follows the common law. Similarly, in the United States, Louisiana has a civil law system, but the remaining states adopt the common law. In India, the state of Goa has a civil law system, but the rest of the country is common law. In China, Hong Kong has a common law system, but the rest of the country has a codified civil law system, strongly influenced by the Napoleonic code. In the European Union, Ireland is the only remaining member state that has an exclusively common law system. However, Cyprus is largely common law, with criminal law based on the civil code, and Malta has a largely civil law system, with common law influence in its public law.

Attempts have been made to codify the common law, most notably by William Blackstone, in his 18th century *Commentaries on the Laws of England*, which were very influential in the development of the legal system of the United States of America. A further attempt was made by Lord Halsbury, in his majestic 31-volume compendium entitled *The Laws of England* (first edition published between 1907 and 1917), which was grandly subtitled 'being a complete statement of the whole law of England'. Much of India's law was codified under British rule in the late 19th century, including the criminal law and contract law. The Indian penal code of 1860 is still the basis for the criminal law in India, Pakistan and Bangladesh.

But the nature of common law is that it evolves, and is resistant to being codified. Common law courts routinely look to the decisions of courts in other common law countries when considering cases.

From the point of view of the expert witness, civil law countries are more likely to use single court-appointed experts. This has the advantage of reducing cost and bias, but increases the danger that the single expert will effectively be the judge on the relevant issue. If the expert makes a mistake, or is biased in favour of one party, there is no other expert to act as a corrective.

Expert witnesses in common law countries are more likely to be appointed by the parties to a case. This means that the parties have the benefit of the expert's advice as the case progresses, but there is a danger that the expert will become too wedded to the client's position to give a truly objective expert view. In an adversarial system, the court would expect that the expert on the other side would be able to correct any misleading evidence.

This book is limited to the principles that apply to expert evidence in common law countries. It will be noted, however, that some hearings in common law countries – notably inquests – are more inquisitorial than adversarial. Furthermore, the courts in many common law countries are tending to treat expert evidence as a separate type of evidence. By introducing new methods such as 'concurrent evidence' (also known as 'hot-tubbing'), judges are increasingly acting in a more inquisitorial manner. Additionally, expert witnesses have duties to the court that go beyond the duties of ordinary witnesses of fact in adversarial hearings.

In practice, expert witnesses do not need to be concerned about whether the hearing is under a common law or civil law system. What matters more is that experts understand their functions, their duties to the court, and the court's requirements at different stages of the procedure.

Chapter 1

Types of Expert and Professional Witness

Many professionals are asked to give evidence in court. Some give largely factual evidence concerning the case at hand. Some impart knowledge from their professional specialisation. Some are asked to express an opinion on a particular issue.

All such professionals are called before the court because they have knowledge, training or experience that sets them apart from the 'layperson'. They are in a privileged position because of their specialised knowledge, and the decision-maker – normally a judge, jury or arbitrator – should be able to rely on that specialised knowledge when deciding the case.

The stereotypical 'expert witness' is a person of great eminence, with extensive experience, who can lecture to the court in impenetrable language about the issue at hand. In reality, evidence is routinely given by professionals from all walks of life, some of whom may have limited experience. Reports are often commissioned concerning an issue in a case, without the writer having to attend court at all.

In this chapter, we look at the role of the professional or expert witness. Although the term 'expert witness' is generally used by the courts, professionals in many fields have a role in court proceedings and may not consider themselves to be 'expert witnesses' as such. In this book, the term 'expert witness' and 'professional witness' is used interchangeably, although the term 'expert witness' may be used more frequently where the opinion of the witness is central to the issue before the court.

Differences between ordinary witnesses and 'expert' or 'professional' witnesses

A large part of a court's function in contested hearings is to determine issues of fact. In order to do this, the court must hear from witnesses who will give evidence of the facts as they know them.

But how do they know these facts? From long experience in every country, the courts have been wary of unreliable witnesses who will testify on oath things that they do not know to be true. This does not necessarily mean that they are lying. They may believe what they are saying to be true, but do not have the necessary grounds to support that belief.

The courts will therefore restrict witnesses to giving evidence only of things they have experienced with their own five senses. They may only tell the court what they have seen or heard (or, less often, felt, smelled or tasted).

The rules of evidence are, of course, far more complicated than this. Every country has developed them in its own way. In the US, the *Federal Rules of Evidence* has been developed to codify its rules. In other countries, the rules have evolved as part of the common law. It is not necessary for an expert witness to understand the rules of evidence in detail. These are matters for the legal team. But it is important that expert and professional witnesses understand how their role differs from that of ordinary witnesses.

Payment

The first difference that is fundamental to the role of the expert and professional witness is one of payment. They are paid for their work concerning the case. While other witnesses of fact may receive witness expenses, they should not profit from their evidence. Otherwise, their evidence might be tainted.

Expert witnesses, on the other hand, may be paid for their work on a particular case. Many cases will involve a considerable amount of work by the specialist involved, both in primary investigations and in professional research. As professionals should not have a direct involvement in the case themselves, they are entitled to be properly paid for this work.

Hearsay evidence

A second difference concerns hearsay evidence. As outlined above, ordinary witnesses of fact should restrict their evidence to the experience of their own senses. They should not give evidence of matters they have heard from other people. There are many reasons for this. The first is that the person who originally spoke the words is not in the witness box, so cannot be compelled by oath or declaration to tell the truth, and cannot be cross-examined. The second is that, from long experience, the courts know that such evidence is unreliable. The original speaker of the words may have been mistaken, or lying. The person repeating the words may have misheard them.

Whether or not the hearsay is true, it is not verifiable, and the courts will – as a rule – not accept it into evidence.

There are many exceptions to the rule against hearsay, but the one that concerns us here is how it applies to the evidence of professionals.

Many professionals do give evidence of primary fact. For example, a pathologist in a homicide trial will give detailed evidence concerning the injuries to the victim as documented during a postmortem examination. But professionals routinely give hearsay evidence in two respects: primary fact; and specialist literature.

Hearsay concerning primary facts

Where, for example, a medical practitioner gives evidence concerning an injured party, it is likely that much of the information concerning that party will have been given in consultation. The injured party may have told the practitioner of pain suffered during an accident, or thereafter. The diagnosis and recommended treatment will largely result from the information given by the injured party. In such a case, the general rule is that the professional can only give such evidence of primary fact if it is given in evidence separately by the original witness, or by another witness who can attest to it.

Where an expert witness relies in evidence on a fact that has been given by another person, but that evidence is not given in court, the relevant part of the expert's evidence may be excluded. If the fact is fundamental to the expert's conclusions, the expert's evidence may have to be excluded in its entirety.

If the fact relied on by the professional is one that is disputed by other witnesses of primary fact, the court will have to resolve that dispute before determining whether the expert's opinion can be relied upon. For example, an injured party may have told a doctor that the pain in his shoulder was so bad that he was unable to play sport or do manual work. The doctor may, in good faith, have made a diagnosis and recommended pain relief or physiotherapy. At trial, evidence may be given by a private investigator or other witness suggesting that the injured party had been playing sport or doing manual work. If that evidence was accepted, the diagnosis of the doctor may be fatally undermined.

Hearsay concerning the specialisation of the professional

Where specialist literature is concerned, the professional is entitled to rely on textbooks or journal articles to demonstrate to the court the view of the relevant profession. Such material is hearsay, in that it is factual matter that is outside the direct experience of the witness.

Not only are professionals entitled to rely on such material in evidence, there are many instances where they should do so. Where two professional witnesses give contradictory evidence concerning matters of their specialisation, it is appropriate that they rely on specialist literature in seeking to resolve this.

There is a caveat, however. Expert witnesses should not seek to mislead the court by selective reliance on such literature. The courts rely on such witnesses as persons with training and experience –and with professional reputations to uphold – to give evidence in good faith. They are not giving evidence to help their respective clients to win the case. They are there to assist the court to determine the truth.

Opinion evidence

As with hearsay, an ordinary witness of fact is not entitled to express an opinion in the witness box. What is meant by 'opinion' in everyday speech can vary widely, including: taste in clothes or music; support for a political movement or idea; or whether or not a particular person is likeable. These are not normally matters to be given in evidence.

Colloquially, 'opinion' can also mean conjecture as to whether a fact is true or not. For example, it would not be unusual to hear a person say: 'In my opinion, that person is guilty.' Again, for obvious reasons, that sort of conjecture cannot be given by a witness in evidence.

The primary exception to the rule against opinion evidence is that an expert witness is entitled to express an opinion in the witness box (and, by extension, in any report written for the court).

This is not to say, however, that experts are free to express any opinion they wish. As with any witness, they cannot engage in conjecture. But, if they have considered the primary facts in a professional manner, and applied the specialist knowledge of their profession, they are entitled to draw reasoned conclusions or inferences and express them to the judge or jury in the form of opinions.

Preparing an expert report

The final key difference between an expert witness and an ordinary witness is that an expert is almost always required to prepare a report in advance of giving evidence. Often the report is prepared before the action is even started by way of summons or other pleading.

This distinction has become a little blurred in more recent times. In many jurisdictions, ordinary witnesses of fact are required to give witness statements in advance of the hearing of the case. However, these are normally prepared by the legal team following an interview with the witness.

In the case of expert witnesses, the report will normally be their own work, prepared following investigation of the facts of the case and any relevant specialist research.

The expert report is generally the evidence that the expert would be expected to give if called to the witness box. It is prepared with the judge, jury or arbitrator in mind, as it is the evidence that would be given to them if they were called upon to determine the case.

In many cases, however, the action will settle or be discontinued long before it reaches a court hearing. But the expert report can be crucial to the decision by a party as to whether the case is to be pursued or how it is to be pursued.

Summary

In short, a professional witness differs from an ordinary witness of fact in that:

- Professionals are paid for their work concerning the case;
- Professionals can give hearsay evidence concerning the facts of the case if the facts are independently proved by another witness;
- Professionals can give hearsay evidence of literature concerning the specialisation of the profession, if done so in an honest and unbiased manner;
- Professionals can give opinion evidence, providing that any opinion is an honest conclusion derived from the facts of the case and the specialisation of the profession; and
- Professionals are normally expected to provide a detailed report of their likely evidence at an early stage of the case.

Professional witnesses generally

The use of the term 'expert witness' can be misleading. Many people in the course of their profession or occupation are called to give evidence in a variety of cases, or are asked to prepare reports for the benefit of courts. In some jurisdictions, they might be called 'expert witnesses' whereas in others the term is restricted to professionals with a more central role in contentious matters.

In personal injury cases, for example, medical professionals are often called to give evidence concerning the medical background of an injured party. The doctor who treated the patient in an emergency room might be called to write a report or give evidence of the patient's condition on arrival and the treatment received there.

In many places of work or shopping centres, there are engineers or health and safety professionals who will attend the site of an accident to prepare a report on the condition of a machine or work system in the immediate aftermath. They may prepare a report including photographs, sketches or samples that will be used by other professionals to help in determining liability.

In cases concerning the welfare of children, it is common for social workers or similar professionals to provide reports to assist the court to decide, for example, whether one parent or the other should have custody of a child, or – in more extreme circumstances – whether a child should be placed in residential accommodation or foster care.

It should not be forgotten that police officers are also professional witnesses when they give evidence. They are primarily trained in the investigation of crime, to seek out and preserve evidence, and give their testimony in that capacity. While they most commonly give evidence in criminal trials, they can often be asked to testify in civil cases such as those arising from road traffic accidents.

Other professionals are routinely called upon to give evidence in criminal trials. Forensic scientists, pathologists, fingerprint experts, and DNA experts can testify as to matters within their specialisation.

Professional witnesses do not normally need to have any particular qualifications or educational background. In a case concerning traditional building techniques, for example, it might be more appropriate to call as a witness a builder with limited formal education but who had worked on such techniques for several decades, as opposed to somebody who had received training in the subject, but had less practical experience of it.

It is routine for such professionals to give evidence of primary fact concerning matters they have investigated themselves, or uncontentious conclusions reached from those investigations. But where the conclusions are central to the court's determination, more caution is required, both from the witness and the legal team retaining them.

Independent expert witnesses appointed by each party

[T]he opinion of scientific men upon proven facts may be given by men of science within their own science. An expert's opinion is admissible to furnish the Court with scientific information which is likely to be outside the experience and knowledge of a judge or jury.[1]
(R v Turner, Court of Appeal of England and Wales)

The classic 'expert witness' is one whose specialist evidence on a central issue will cause the case to be won or lost.

Where an issue arises for determination that is outside the knowledge of the judge, jury or arbitrator, expert witnesses may be called to assist the court in reaching a decision on that issue. It is important for both the decision maker and the witness to understand their role in reaching the decision. It is the decision maker – judge, jury or arbitrator – who makes the decision. It is the expert who assists by educating the decision maker as to the specialist knowledge. The court cannot – or should not – abdicate its role to that of the expert. Experts should not tell the court their opinion on the matter without explaining how the opinion was reached.

Where the issue is contentious—where two experts have reached different views—the decision will inevitably be a difficult one to determine. Judges, as laypersons, will have to decide the matter based on specialist knowledge that they have had to understand in a short time. Where the matter is to be determined by a jury—the members of which will as a matter of course have varying levels of education—it is necessary for the specialist knowledge to be explained in terms that they will understand.

It will be clear to any reader what the consequences may be if an 'expert witness' presents information in an unclear manner. More seriously, if the witness presents information that is biased, it can – and often does—lead to miscarriages of justice.

For this reason, the courts have set out in many cases the duties of experts who give evidence in contentious matters. These are discussed in more detail in the next chapter.

Single joint experts (or court-appointed experts)

The cost of expert evidence can be extremely high, so the courts often try to limit the issues that require two professionals, acting in an adversarial manner. There may be some issues that can be determined by a single expert. If the parties can agree on such an expert, the report can be written by him or her for both sides. Alternatively, one of the parties may apply to the court to appoint a single expert, or the court can appoint such an expert 'of its own motion' (i.e. on the initiative of the judge).

As with any expert, the single joint expert should give evidence in an independent manner. The danger, however, is that the expert does not have the 'supervision' of an expert from the other side. It is common for one of the parties to be unhappy with the evidence given, and then to seek to appoint another expert to advise on the issue. The courts will generally have procedures to deal with such a situation.

Assessors

In some types of case, the court will sit with an 'assessor'. This is an independent expert who sits with the judge to explain any technical evidence given.

The danger of assessors, from the point of view of the parties, is that the parties will not be in a position to supervise the conversations that take place between the assessor and the judge when the court is not sitting.

Sometimes, the assessor is required to provide a report to set out the advice given to the judge, so that the parties can see the basis of the judge's decisions on technical issues.

Although assessors sit with the judge, they should not seek to supplant the role of the judge by imposing a decision, nor should judges abdicate their own role as decision makers. The assessor should advise the judge on the relevant issue or issues, and the judge should understand the issues before making the decision.

'Ad hoc' use of experts to filter primary evidence

An issue that increasingly arises, as a result of developments in technology, is that the quantity of evidence can be too much for any court to handle on its own. It needs to be inspected by an independent professional in order to establish what is relevant.

To date, this issue has arisen primarily in criminal trials, with close-circuit television (CCTV) footage.[2] It would not be practical for a jury to be shown several hours of CCTV footage, so a police officer might watch all the footage in order to select the parts considered to be relevant. This can be unsatisfactory from the accused's point of view, unless another similar professional has an opportunity to inspect all the footage as well. The police officer may have failed to disclose material that could be of assistance to the defence team.

In civil trials, teams of lawyers are often employed to comb through documents disclosed in electronic discovery. However, if documents of a highly specialised nature are disclosed in large quantities, it can be necessary to employ a suitably qualified professional to consider them all. In theory, it would be possible for the legal teams to agree that the material could be considered by a single independent professional. In practice, each team is likely to be wary that something of benefit to its own side might be overlooked. Similar issues may arise in 'white collar' prosecutions, where large quantities of financial documents are disclosed and have to be considered.

The use of experts 'ad hoc' to filter the primary evidence opened to the court is likely to remain controversial. Nonetheless, with the expansion of evidentiary material resulting from technological developments, it will not be practical to conduct plenary hearings with oral evidence if some sort of filtering system is not developed. The use of suitably qualified experts may be the only reasonable solution.

Interpreters and translators

> An interpreter should be suitably qualified and aware of his or her responsibilities to ensure accuracy and objectivity in the provision of interpretation services.[3] (*R v Foronda*, Court of Appeal of Northern Ireland)

Although not strictly 'witnesses', it is worth mentioning the role of interpreters and translators in the court process, as their expertise is relied upon by the decision maker in determining the truth.

A translator is a person who translates documents from another language into the language of the court.

An interpreter is a person who gives a simultaneous translation of the spoken word from the witness to the court and—where necessary—from the court to one of the parties to the case.

People who appear before the court are entitled to understand the court proceedings, and to be understood when they give evidence. Where their habitual language does not include the primary language of the court, the right to a translator or interpreter is fundamental.

11

Interpreters and translators are generally required to make an oath or declaration similar to that of a witness.

In the *Foronda* case, quoted above, an interpreter for the prosecution heard an interpreter for the defence speak to the witness in a dialect that the prosecution interpreter did not understand. It was suspected that the interpreter was prompting the witness to give a particular answer to the question asked. The judge said:

> Private or whispered conversations between an interpreter and a witness giving evidence are inappropriate since they generate a real risk of unidentifiable error, the risk of a complaint about lack of objectivity on the part of the interpreter and may undermine the principle of open and transparent justice.

In principle, an interpreter or translator may be cross-examined as to the quality of the translation. In practice, this rarely happens.

While interpreters and translators are not witnesses, they are experts in that they have specialist knowledge that is relied upon by the court to resolve the case. As with expert witnesses, they are relied upon to act a professional manner in all their dealings with the court.

Conclusion

Whatever role professionals have in court proceedings, whether writing reports, giving evidence, providing notes, advising the judge, sorting through copious evidential material, or translating documents, their primary duties are to assist the court in determining the truth. In the next chapter, we consider the nature of the duties of professional or expert witnesses.

Notes

[1] *R v Turner* [1975] 1 All ER 70.
[2] See, in particular, the case of *R v Clare* [1995] 2 Cr App R 333.
[3] Coghlin LJ in *R v Foronda* [2014] NICA 17.

Chapter 2

The Duties of Expert or Professional Witnesses

On 12 April 1985, at about 11pm, a ship called the Ikarian Reefer ran aground off the coast of Sierra Leone. Two hours later, a fire broke out in the engine room and the crew quickly abandoned ship. The owners of the ship, National Justice Compania Naviera SA, claimed against their insurer, Prudential Assurance Co Ltd, in respect of the loss. The insurers refused cover, taking the view that the ship had been deliberately scuttled. The owners sued the insurers in the High Court of England and Wales, and, as the ship was insured at a value of £3 million, each side retained a large number of expert witnesses to support their case. To quote the Court of Appeal, the experts had a 'field day'. Thirty-two days of hearing were devoted to the fire alone, which arose from an open fuel tap on the line of the diesel tank.

In his appropriately lengthy judgment, Mr Justice Cresswell sought to resolve the enormous amount of expert evidence before him. Taking the view that some experts had not complied with the requirements of the court, he set out a number of principles concerning expert evidence, drawn from earlier case law. These are widely viewed as authoritative principles on the duties of expert evidence and have been cited with apparent approval in the courts of Canada, Australia, New Zealand, Ireland, India, South Africa and other common law countries. However, Mr Justice Cresswell did not suggest that they were definitive or exhaustive. These principles are set out in an appendix to this volume.[1]

At the conclusion of the trial, Mr Justice Cresswell concluded that the Ikarian Reefer had not been deliberately run aground, but that there had been negligence on the part of the Master of the ship. He held that the insurers had failed to establish that the ship had been deliberately set on fire. If the ship had been deliberately set on fire by one of the crew, it was an act of 'barratry' that was covered by the insurance policy if not done in connivance with the owners. Accordingly, the owners were entitled to the benefit of the insurance policy.

On appeal, the Court of Appeal approved the list of duties of expert witnesses, but took the view that Mr Justice Cresswell had drawn impermissible inferences from the experts in the case:

> When the Judge was reviewing the evidence in relation to the various theories put forward, he expressed the view in every case where there was any conflict of opinion between the experts, that he preferred the views of the owners' experts. He gave no specific reason for doing so, other than the general matters to which he had already referred. We find it somewhat remarkable that honest, distinguished, experienced and qualified experts called on behalf of the Defence in relation to the fire should always be wrong, while those called on behalf of the Plaintiffs should always be right.

The appeal court engaged in a detailed examination of the evidence and concluded that the ship had been deliberately run aground by the Master. Lord Justice Stuart Smith further commented:

> As for the experts in relation to the fire, the owners' experts put forward immensely complex theories to try and afford an innocent explanation of the fire and the open tap. These were based on the most tenuous evidence, or no evidence at all, but rather assumptions.[2]

The High Court's decision was set aside.

In the later case of *Anglo Group plc v Winther Brown and Co Ltd*,[3] the High Court adopted the list of duties as set out in *The Ikarian Reefer*, but updated them in accordance with more recent rules adopted by the courts of England and Wales in 1996, known as the 'Woolf Reforms'.[4] Despite the English focus of the Woolf Reforms, the restated list of duties has met with broad approval in Canada and Ireland, and it is reasonable to say that it broadly reflects common law principles on the duties of expert witnesses.[5]

However, the list of duties as set out in *The Ikarian Reefer*, and *Anglo*

Group plc. do not cover all duties expected of expert witnesses, and may have been written more with lawyers in mind than the expert witnesses themselves. In this chapter, the duties expected of experts are broken down and discussed in turn.

1. To tell the truth, both in written reports and in oral evidence

> There may of course be cases where an expert witness, who has prepared a report, could not go into the witness-box and assert that his report contained the truth, the whole truth and nothing but the truth without some qualification. In that case it may well be that the substance of his evidence has not been disclosed and that the qualification ought to have been either in the report or disclosed separately. In my experience no reputable expert would sign such a report without putting the qualification in it. But I do not think that an expert witness, or any other witness, obliges himself to volunteer his views on every issue in the whole case when he takes an oath to tell the whole truth. What he does oblige himself to do is to tell the whole truth about those matters which he is asked about.[6] (*Derby & Co Ltd v Weldon*, High Court of England and Wales)

In June 2017, it was reported that a number of expert witnesses had been imprisoned in the UK for fabricating evidence. The experts were employees of a company called Autofocus Ltd, who provided expert witness services for insurance companies. They were specifically used to challenge car hire rates claimed by people who sought compensation for replacement vehicles after road traffic accidents. In six cases, the experts knowingly gave false evidence on oath. In a private prosecution for contempt of court brought by a car hire company, it was established that 30,000 cases had been affected by reports written by the experts. The judge hearing the case above described it as perjury 'on an industrial scale'. Seven of the experts were imprisoned, for terms between six months and 13 months.[7]

Almost everybody knows that when a witness enters the box to give evidence, an oath, affirmation or declaration is made to tell 'the truth, the whole truth, and nothing but the truth'. Where a person knowingly misleads the court having made such a declaration, that person can face criminal prosecution for the offence of perjury.

It should come as no surprise that the same duty to tell the truth in court, applies to expert witnesses just as much as it applies to any other witness. When a judge, jury or arbitrator hears evidence, they need to be able to rely on it. It is not uncommon to find witnesses of fact who will exaggerate, or sometimes flagrantly lie, when giving their evidence. Where this happens, the court needs to rely on other factual sources, such as photographs or contemporaneous documents, to decide which witness of fact is likely to be telling the truth. If there are no such sources, the court will simply have to rely on which witness appears most credible, having considered all of the evidence.

Where professionals give evidence, it is generally expected that they will tell the truth. As persons of standing in the community, with reputations to protect, it is unlikely that they will tell outright lies. However, as people who are retained—and paid—by one of the parties, there is a danger that they will put a 'gloss' on some of their evidence to assist their own side.

Professional witnesses may be less familiar with the requirement to tell the truth in reports prepared for court proceedings. After all, many reports are never read by a judge, as the cases are resolved before they reach a court.

But it is the fact that the reports are often not read by a decision maker that makes the requirement of truth so important. If reports are prepared for either side that exaggerate the case of the injured party, or exaggerate the defence of the alleged wrongdoer, this may be designed to increase their 'bargaining power'. Only if the writer is cross-examined in court will the report's shortcomings become apparent. In the meantime, each side could be negotiating in the belief that their case is stronger than it actually is. Given the time and expense involved in calling experts to give evidence, and face cross-examination, the courts do not wish them to be encouraged to overstate their clients' case.

In the UK, expert reports are now required to include a 'statement of truth', which elevates the report to the status of a sworn affidavit, in that the writers may face prosecution if they are found to have deliberately included an incorrect statement.

A recent example of such a prosecution concerned a GP in a low-value personal injuries case. His initial report stated that the injured party had recovered from the injuries. This statement was queried by the solicitor, and the GP rewrote the report without consulting again with the injured party. In the rewritten report, the GP stated that the injured party was likely to recover within a few months. When the altered report came to light, the GP was prosecuted for contempt of court. He was given a suspended sentence, but the Court of Appeal said that a term of between nine and twelve months imprisonment would have been appropriate.[8]

> If you are asked to prepare a report, or to give evidence, you should ensure that it is truthful as to:
> * your qualifications
> * the facts of the case
> * any specialist or technical information
> * any conclusions you have reached
> * and any other relevant matters.

2. To be independent of the client and legal team

> While some degree of consultation between experts and legal advisers is entirely proper, it is necessary that expert evidence presented to the court should be, and should be seen to be, the independent product of the expert, uninfluenced as to form or content by the exigencies of litigation. To the extent that it is not, the evidence is likely to be not only incorrect but self-defeating.[9] (*Whitehouse v Jordan*, United Kingdom House of Lords)

> Expert witnesses have a special duty to the court to provide fair, objective and non-partisan assistance. A proposed expert witness who is unable or unwilling to comply with this duty is not qualified to give expert opinion evidence and should not be permitted to do so.[10]
> (*White Burgess Langille Inman v Abbott and Haliburton Co Ltd*, Supreme Court of Canada)

It is never the job of professional witnesses to assist their client to win the case. A witness should not adopt the role of an advocate.

This can seem counterintuitive. In normal circumstances, it is the job of professionals to get the best result for their clients. If employed as a medical practitioner, the job is to help the client get better. If employed as an architect, the job is to help the client get the building that the client is looking for. Furthermore, the expert is being paid by the client. Why should the expert not seek to help the client win?

The answer is that the primary duty of the expert witness—as with any witness—is to the court, to assist the decision maker in determining the truth. No witness is expected to give partial evidence. Because expert witnesses have greater latitude in giving hearsay and opinion evidence, they are expected to uphold the highest standards of their profession in their assistance to the court. They are not 'guns for hire'.

Having said this, there can be no doubt that the duty of independence is often misunderstood (or, to put it less charitably, ignored). In fact, in almost every high-profile miscarriage of justice, there has been a flagrant breach by expert witnesses of their duty of independence, and the tainted evidence has been relied upon to secure the wrongful conviction.

In the Dreyfus affair in the 1890s, the prosecution in France relied on handwriting 'experts' to give false evidence that it was Dreyfus who had written a note giving secret military information to the German embassy. It was later conclusively established that the note had been written by another officer by the name of Esterhazy, who had not even disguised his handwriting in the original note; however, the handwriting 'experts' maintained their position long after it should have been rejected. In the cases of the Birmingham Six, the Guildford Four and Judith Ward, forensic evidence was presented to prove that the accused persons had handled explosives. The tests used were ambiguous at best, and could not have grounded such a conclusion 'beyond reasonable doubt', but the convictions were not set aside for decades. In the case of Sally Clark, a woman who had lost two children to cot deaths, questionable statistical evidence was given by a paediatrician to establish the unlikelihood of two cot deaths in one family, and a pathologist withheld evidence that might have led to an acquittal.

There can be little doubt that in countries where the death penalty exists, many people have been wrongfully executed on foot of questionable expert evidence.

On a lighter note, some expert witnesses have sought to downplay their own obligations to the court. In a 1995 English case, it came to light that an architect giving evidence as an expert witness had written an article entitled: 'The Expert Witness: Partisan with a Conscience'. In the article, he compared the role of the expert witness to a huckster working a 'Three Card Trick':

> If by an analogous 'sleight of mind' an expert witness is able so to present the data that they seem to suggest an interpretation favourable to the side instructing him, that is, it seems to me, within the rules of our particular game, even if it means playing down or omitting some material consideration.

Mr Justice Laddie of the High Court of England and Wales was not amused:

> The function of a court of law is to discover the truth relating to the issues before it. In doing that it has to assess the evidence adduced by the parties. The judge is not a rustic who has chosen to play a game of Three Card Trick. He is not fair game. Nor is the truth.[11]

In criminal trials, where the standard of proof is 'beyond a reasonable doubt', it should be self-evident that experts giving evidence for the prosecution should be scrupulously impartial. If their evidence is presented in a manner calculated to assist the prosecution, it could give rise to a wrongful conviction.

But miscarriages of justice may also occur in civil actions. In almost every trial, something valuable is at stake for at least one of the parties. In many it is a matter of money, but it could lead to one of the parties losing their house. If a wrongfully injured person was to lose a personal injuries case, they might not be able to afford the necessary medical or nursing care. In family law cases, a biased report by a childcare professional could lead to one parent losing access to their children.

The duty of independence has two practical implications: the first concerns conflicts of interest; the second is that the witness should not act, or be seen to act, as a member of the legal team.

Conflicts of interest

A professional who is asked to participate in court proceedings should disclose any potential conflicts of interest.

A conflict of interest is any external connection with one of the parties that might lead the expert witness to want to assist that party's case. Conflicts of interest largely boil down to personal connections and financial interest. If, for example, the expert has a large shareholding in a company that is part of the litigation, this should be disclosed. If the expert is related to one of the parties, this should also be disclosed. In either case, it is likely to be considered preferable for the expert not to give evidence.

It can be difficult to avoid perceived conflicts of interest. If the expert had, for example, worked under contract for one of the parties more than ten years before any involvement in the litigation, and had never met any of the personnel relevant to the case, it may be the case that the connection would not be of such a magnitude as to affect the expert's sympathies. If the connection is disclosed at the outset, the parties cannot object to it at a later date. However, if the connection is discovered during the litigation, after the expert has worked on the case for some time, one of the parties may seek to raise the matter before the court to suggest that the expert was not an appropriate person to act in the case. The objection would be to the non-disclosure rather than the connection itself.

In general, the courts take a pragmatic view of such connections. If the expert discloses the connection, and there is no other reason to impugn his professional conduct, an objection to his acting in the case will probably not be sustained.

Experts and their instructing legal teams should not, however, be blind to the fact that the very retainer of the expert creates a conflict of interest. To be retained by the party in itself gives rise to a sense that the expert is part of the 'team'. Where, as often happens, a company retains the same expert for several cases, personal connections will develop with the company's personnel and legal advisors. Furthermore, the expert is likely to want to continue working for the same company in future cases, which gives rise to a further financial incentive to help the company succeed.

This gives rise to the second practical implication, which is that the witness should not act, or be seen to act, as a member of the legal team.

The witness should not act, or be seen to act, as a member of the legal team

No suggestion should be made by the lawyers that the expert should come to any particular conclusion, nor should the expert ask what answer to a particular question would be the most helpful.

All correspondence and consultations should adopt an 'arms length' tone. Different countries have different rules on disclosure of documents, but it would be unfortunate if an expert had prepared a meticulous report, but sent it to the legal team under cover of an e-mail saying 'This should blow their case out of the water!'

Similarly, consultations between the expert and legal team should be treated as an exchange of information. The legal team may ask searching and detailed questions about the report and its conclusions, or the answers likely to be given by other experts in the case, but the team should not attempt to influence the substance of the report or the likely evidence. Witnesses, for their part, should not be involved in discussions of litigation strategy.

Your role as an expert or professional witness is to be impartial. You should not seek to assist the client to win the case. You should disclose any conflicts of interest to the instructing legal team and, if you are not satisfied that you can act impartially, you should refuse to accept the instructions. If the client or legal team seek to persuade you to give testimony that is not your honest and truthful view, you should refuse. If this leads to a conflict with them, you should consider whether to consult your professional body, or take independent legal advice.

3. To give evidence within their own expertise

An expert witness should make it clear when a particular question or issue falls outside his expertise.[12] (*The Ikarian Reefer*, High Court of England and Wales)

In 2007, the well-known Irish jockey Kieren Fallon was charged in the UK with race-fixing, along with five other people. The allegation was that they had broken the rules of the Jockey Club by stopping horses racing on their merits. The prosecution called Ray Murrihy, who was the chief steward of New South Wales, as expert witness. During the course of the trial, it became clear that Mr Murrihy was well-versed in the rules that applied in Australia. However, in evidence, he admitted: 'It was not incumbent that I verse myself in UK or other jurisdiction rules.' In dismissing the charges, the judge commented: 'This is an extraordinary admission given that he was purporting to give evidence about 27 races run in the UK according to UK racing rules.'[13]

A similar issue arose in an Indian case in the 1980s. The disease of Apple Scab had affected the apple crop in the mountainous state of Himachal Pradesh. The State government established a scheme whereby the government would compensate farmers for their diseased fruit if they delivered it for destruction. Schemes like this are always prone to corruption, especially if there is collusion between administrators of the scheme and those likely to benefit. Allegations of this sort arose, and a number of apple farmers were prosecuted for criminal conspiracy and convicted. On appeal, it transpired that the expert witness for the prosecution, a man with extensive training in agriculture, had given evidence concerning the maximum capacity of apple trees, and based his testimony on statistics showing that some farmers had claimed for more than their trees could have produced. The Supreme Court of India commented:

> [the expert] has not stated anything in his testimony to show that he had made any scientific study or research in assessing the productivity of apple trees in the State of Himachal Pradesh. He does not even state whether he had undertaken any such work prior to the present case. No doubt as an officer of the Horticulture Department of the State Government he might have acquired some experience in the matter but that is not sufficient to make him an expert in the field and to give the label of 'expert evidence' to his testimony.[14]

It can be difficult to establish what sort of expertise is required in a particular case, or what level of specialisation. A general medical practitioner knows considerably more about, for example, heart disease than a layperson, but considerably less than a heart specialist. In a particular case, the central question may lie within the experience or training of experts, but there may be tangential issues that they are less qualified to comment upon.

Therefore, expert witnesses who are approached to act in a case, should consider carefully whether the issues are within the relevant specialisation. If they are outside the experts' particular field of study, they should not accept the instructions. If the issues are broadly within their expertise, but likely to raise other issues, they should warn the instructing legal team.

When preparing the initial report (or any subsequent reports), the expert should make it clear whether any issue arises that should be examined by somebody with a different specialisation. This does not mean that writers of reports cannot comment on the issue as far as their own expertise is relevant, but they should not seek to reach a definitive conclusion on a matter outside of their training or experience.

When taking instructions from the client or legal team, you should ensure that the issues are within your expertise. If, at any stage of the case, you take the view that there are matters that are outside your expertise, you should inform the client or legal team. In your report or evidence, if you are commenting on matters outside your expertise, you should make this clear.

4. To assist the court (or other decision maker) to reach its own decision

> It is the duty of an expert witness to provide material on which a court can form its own conclusions on relevant issues.[15] (*Kennedy v Cordia*, Supreme Court of the United Kingdom)

> [A] court should not blindly accept and act upon the evidence of an expert witness ... but must decide for itself whether it can safely accept the expert's opinion.[16] (*R v Nksatlala*, Supreme Court of South Africa)

The relationship between the expert and the decision maker must be understood by all parties. The decision maker should not simply defer to the expert on any contentious issue without understanding how the expert reached the relevant conclusion. Similarly, the expert should not present a bald conclusion without explaining it in a manner that the court understands.

Depending on the type of hearing, the decision maker may be a judge, a jury or an arbitrator. In other hearings, the decision maker could be a panel or even a parliamentary committee. In professional disciplinary proceedings, with extensive powers to curtail the ability of a professional person to continue in practice, the decision maker may be a 'fitness to practice' committee.

Because decision makers can vary from judges, who are generally experienced legal professionals, to juries, who are generally laypersons drawn at random from the community, to specialists in other fields, the manner in which the expert evidence is presented may also vary.

Experts should probably approach each decision maker in the

manner in which they would advise a new client. No knowledge of the subject should be assumed, but the expert should explain the technical material in a manner that enables the decision maker to make an informed decision.

There are two relevant legal principles. The first is what is known as the 'common knowledge rule'. This is the principle that expert evidence should not be relied upon if the decision maker can make the decision based on common knowledge. It may be that the expert has conducted a very useful factual investigation that the decision maker can rely upon, but that any further comment or expression of opinion is superfluous.

The second principle is known as the 'ultimate issue rule'. It is sometimes said that an expert witness should not express an opinion on the 'ultimate issue' in a case. This is probably an over-simplification. In a criminal trial, for example, fingerprint experts should never tell the jury they are of the opinion that the accused person is guilty. Nor should they even express a view that the accused person was at the scene of the crime. If the accused's fingerprints closely match a fingerprint found at the scene, this should be relayed to the jury, and it will be for them to determine whether this leads them to conclude that the accused was at the scene of the crime, and—taken together with the other evidence—whether the person is guilty.

On the other hand, a medical negligence action may turn entirely on whether the defendant's actions fell below the standard to be expected of a member of the medical profession. Experts on either side will be asked to give their opinion on the defendant's conduct in the case. The 'ultimate issue' in the case is the standard of care. Each expert will be asked in searching detail of their view of the defendant's conduct, but it will be for the decision maker in the case to conclude whether the allegation of negligence is upheld.

The substance of the expert evidence on which the decision maker will make the decision is broken down in to three parts: i. the facts of the case; ii. the expertise of the profession; and iii. the opinion or conclusion drawn by the witness having applied the expertise to the facts. Because there is some controversy concerning 'opinion evidence', we shall address that issue first.

> Your role as an expert or professional witness is not to tell the court the answer. It is to explain matters to the court in such a way that the court can reach its own decision.

5. To reach a reasoned conclusion on the issues

[A]n expert's opinion represents his reasoned conclusion based on certain facts or data, which are either common cause, or established by his own evidence or that of some other competent witness. Except possibly where it is not controverted, an expert's bald statement of his opinion is not of any real assistance. Proper evaluation of the opinion can only be undertaken if the process of reasoning which led to the conclusion, including the premises from which the reasoning proceeds, are disclosed by the expert.[17] (*Coopers (South Africa) (Pty) Ltd v Deutsche Gesellschaft für Schädlingsbekämpfung mbH*, Supreme Court of South Africa)

An expert must explain the basis of his or her evidence when it is not personal observation or sensation; mere assertion or '*bare ipse dixit*' [unproven statement] carries little weight ... If anything, the suggestion that an unsubstantiated *ipse dixit* carries little weight is understated; in our view such evidence is worthless.[18]

(*Kennedy v Cordia*, Supreme Court of the United Kingdom)

One of the key differences between an expert or professional witness and an ordinary witness of fact is that an ordinary witness is not allowed to express an opinion in the witness box. The facts of the case should be presented to the judge or jury, and it will be for them to draw the appropriate inferences.

Where an expert gives evidence, this will be for the particular reason that a judge or jury cannot make the decision without expert assistance. In order to assist the judge or jury, the expert will need to have drawn inferences from the evidence, and be in a position to explain them to the court.

Therefore, the primary exception to the rule against 'opinion evidence' is that experts can express an opinion. But this does not mean that their evidence solely consists of an expression of opinion. Furthermore, it does not give experts *carte blanche* to express an opinion that has not been reached by the appropriate professional process.

Rather than use the term 'opinion', it would be safer to say that experts can express 'reasoned conclusions' on the relevant issue or issues. Not only should experts be in a position to explain why they have reached the conclusions expressed to the court, they should be in a position to address conclusions put forward by other experts – or that are likely to be put forward – and explain why they prefer their own view.

> Any conclusions you reach in your report should be based solidly on the verifiable facts of the case and the established standards of your profession. They should be your professional opinion rather than your personal view.

6. To research or ascertain the relevant facts

> If the expert's opinion is not properly researched because he considers that insufficient data is available, then he must say so and indicate that his opinion is no more than a provisional one.[19] (*Re J (Child Abuse: Expert Evidence)*, High Court of England and Wales)

> It is my strongly held view that where a witness purports to give evidence in a professional capacity as an expert witness, he owes a duty to ascertain all the surrounding facts and to give that evidence in the context of those facts, whether they support the proposition which he is being asked to put forward or not.[20] (*Fitzpatrick v DPP*, High Court of Ireland)

When expert witnesses are instructed by a solicitor or client, it is likely that they will be presented with a summary of the facts of the case. It may be that the solicitor will ask the expert to provide a preliminary view to establish whether there is a case worth pursuing. There is nothing to prevent experts from providing such a preliminary opinion, providing that the opinion states clearly that it is based on facts as presented by the instructing solicitor.

However, if the matter were to proceed further, experts must be provided with the means to establish whether these facts are true. In many cases, expert or professional witnesses have a key role in establishing primary facts.

For example, in a homicide case, or any case involving an unexplained death, a pathologist will need to examine the body of the deceased. In the course of this examination, information will need to be assembled to establish any of the possible causes of death. This exercise should be conducted in a strictly neutral manner. It is not the job of a pathologist simply to find whatever evidence may assist the prosecution in securing a conviction. Not only should the information be assembled from the examination, it should be disclosed to all parties. As this is primary evidence, it must be made available to the other pathologists, to see what inferences may be drawn from it.

In cases involving allegations of medical negligence, the experts need to consider the contemporaneous notes concerning the care of the injured party. It may also be necessary to carry out an examination of the injured party, or interview them about the care they received.

In construction cases, it is generally necessary for the experts to attend on site to examine the alleged defects to the building, both to establish how they arose and how they may be remedied. Again, this is an exercise in assembling primary facts. If two experts attend at the same site, and carry out similar inspections (including measurements and photographs), there should not be any substantial dispute as to the primary facts.

In some cases, legal issues will arise as to whether experts have sufficient access to the necessary factual information or material. For example, in the 2000 Canadian case of *Jacobson v Sveen*, a plaintiff in a personal injuries action refused to hand over her medical reports to the defence team in advance of a neurological examination. The Court of Queen's Bench in the State of Alberta concluded that the defence was entitled to see the report in order to conduct a proper examination:

The plaintiff has put her medical condition in issue. Therefore, the defence is entitled to make its own assessment of her medical condition and is also entitled to her medical evidence. The plaintiff is entitled, after receipt of the defendant's neurological report, to have additional neurological examinations undertaken; the defendants, on the other hand, are unlikely to be allowed a second neurological examination merely because the plaintiff has obtained an additional report of that type. The plaintiff will also be entitled, at trial, to challenge the opinions of the defence medical experts. And she is entitled to expect that experts will give unbiased and honest evidence in court and that if the expert takes on the role of an advocate the judge will diminish the weight of that expert's opinion accordingly. She is not unfairly treated by this process.[21]

Where experts take the view that they cannot prepare a proper report without inspecting documents or matters in the possession of one of the other parties, this should be communicated to the legal team which should seek to facilitate it.

It may be that case that the inspection by experts will establish an inconsistency with the instructions they have been given. Clients at times have faulty memories. Sometimes they tell deliberate untruths. It is not the job of the experts to cover up any inconsistencies, nor is it their job to expose deceit. The inconsistencies should be set out as clearly as possible, and it will be for the legal team to decide how to deal with them.

> If you are asked to prepare an expert report, make sure that you have access to the necessary factual material. If any of your conclusions are based solely on information you have been provided by the client or legal team that you have not been able to corroborate, this should be made clear to the reader and, in evidence, to the court.

7. To educate the decision maker as to the relevant specialist or technical knowledge

Their primary function is to educate the court in the technology – they come as teachers, as makers of the mantle for the court to don. For that purpose it does not matter whether they do or do not approximate to the skilled man. What matters is how good they are at explaining things.[22] (*Rockwater v Technip France*, Court of Appeal of England and Wales)

> Their duty is to furnish the Judge or jury with the necessary scientific criteria for testing the accuracy of their conclusions, so as to enable the Judge or jury to form their own independent judgment by the application of these criteria to the facts proved in evidence. The scientific opinion evidence, if intelligible, convincing and tested, becomes a factor (and often an important factor) for consideration along with the whole other evidence in the case, but the decision is for the judge or jury.[23] (*Davie v Magistrates of Edinburgh*, Court of Session of Scotland)

In the 2001 Australian case of *Makita (Australia) Pty Ltd v Sprowles*,[24] the Court of Appeal of New South Wales considered an accident where the plaintiff had fallen on a stairway that she regularly used on her way to work. The injuries were so serious that the Supreme Court had awarded her AUS$1.5 million in damages. The plaintiff's evidence was that her foot 'went out' from underneath her. A physicist who specialised in the investigation of slipping accidents conducted an examination of the stairway, nine years after the accident itself, and concluded that it had been slippery. At the time of the accident, there had been no national standard for slip resistance in floors, but such a standard had been introduced by the time of the appeal. The problem for the plaintiff was that the stairway, even nine years after the accident, did meet the national standard for slip resistance (AS 3661.1:1993). The expert sought to persuade the court that the national standard was not an adequate test, but the court was not sympathetic:

> [The expert]'s view would appear to be that meeting the standard laid down in AS 3661.1:1993 is not an adequate test of whether or not the surface of a floor is slip resistant and that the only way to determine whether or not a surface is, or is not, to be regarded as safe is by having regard to the coefficient of friction of the surface of the floor and the coefficient of friction of the type of sole actually, or likely to be, worn by those walking on the surface; if this is a correct assessment of [the expert]'s view then it is quite impossible to reconcile that view with the existence of an Australian Standard, and [the expert], in my opinion, has provided no defensible reason for his view being preferred to that standard.

In the relevant area of expertise, the judge is a layperson. The expert is a specialist. The expert is only required because the judge does not have the requisite specialist knowledge, but the judge has to make the decision with the benefit of the expertise. So there is a heavy burden on the expert to explain the specialist knowledge in a way that the judge (or jury or arbitrator) will understand.

Experts obtain their specialist knowledge in a number of ways: their initial professional education; their apprenticeship or training; their ongoing professional experience; and 'continuing professional development'.

A common fault among expert witnesses is that they attempt to rely solely or primarily on opinions derived from their own professional experience, when this should be only one consideration – and arguably the least important.

Take, for example, an accident in the workplace. An engineer retained by the employee tells the court that, in his opinion, the work practice was inherently unsafe, based on his 15 years of examining similar systems. An engineer for the employer tells the court that, in her opinion based on her 20 years of examining similar systems, it was a perfectly safe system and that the accident was entirely the fault of the employee.

For courts to decide whether the system was safe, they can either choose the evidence of the more experienced engineer, or the one that sounds more plausible, or ignore the conclusions of either side and decide the case based on the courts' own opinion. Neither expert will have been of great assistance in deciding the central question.

But experts are not there to give evidence of their own personal view. They are there to explain to the court the specialist knowledge of their profession. Therefore, in the case of the workplace accident, each engineer should consider the relevant literature on the subject. There is extensive health and safety guidance as to most types of manual work, which should assist the court in determining whether the work practice was inherently unsafe. As in the Australian case above, there are often national standards that apply to the case. If each engineer presents this information in a frank and unbiased manner, not only will it be of more value to the court, it is less likely that the experts will be in a position to contradict each other.

If, for some reason, there are no textbooks that address the subject, no national standards, and no other guidance, the experts should try to find comparable work practices to show whether a court can assess the relevant practice objectively.

While textbooks and technical literature are 'hearsay', in that they are statements by third parties that are introduced to prove the truth of their contents, most countries have rules that specifically allow witnesses to introduce such literature. In the US, this is referred to as the 'learned treatises' exception to the hearsay rule.

> If you are asked to prepare an expert report, make sure that you refer to the applicable professional standards in reaching your conclusion. If these are complicated, it is your job to explain them in language that an educated layperson will understand. You should ensure that your conclusions are objectively justifiable from a professional point of view, and not based solely on your personal experience.

8. To co-operate with the client and instructing legal team

It is not in dispute that an expert who acts in civil litigation owes his client a duty to act with reasonable skill and care. He owes this duty in contract ... and in tort ... He holds himself out as a skilled and competent person. The client relies on his advice in determining whether to bring or defend proceedings, in considering settlement values and in appraising the risks at trial. The client also relies on him to give the court skilled and competent expert opinion evidence.[25] (*Jones v Kaney*, Supreme Court of the United Kingdom)

As a matter of principle, the circumstances in which an expert is retained to provide litigation or arbitration support services could give rise to a relationship of trust and confidence. In common with counsel and solicitors, an independent expert owes duties to the court that may not align with the interests of the client. However, as with counsel and solicitors, the paramount duty owed to the court is not inconsistent with an additional duty of loyalty to the client. ... [T]he terms of the expert's appointment will encompass that paramount duty to the court. Therefore, there is no conflict between the duty that the expert owes to his client and the duty that he owes to the court.[26] (*A v B*, High Court of England and Wales)

It should be clear at this stage that the primary duty of the expert witness is to the court—the judge, jury, arbitrator or other decision maker—to assist it in reaching an informed decision on the relevant technical issues. This duty overrides any duty to the client who is paying their fee, or to the instructing legal team.

But the expert still has a duty to the client and legal team. They will rely on the expert's report in deciding whether to pursue the case at all, or in deciding how it will be pursued. In many cases, they will be the only ones to read the expert's report if the case is discontinued, or if it is settled at an early stage before the reports are exchanged. At each stage, they must be in a position to know what the expert would be likely to say on the relevant issues if called to give evidence.

While some experts may be too eager to establish a case for their client, they would also be at fault if they were too cautious. If they wrongly took the view that their client had a weak case, the client might not pursue a claim that they were entitled to win.

The expert also has an ongoing duty to the team to answer questions arising from the report or reports they have furnished. Just as the judge needs to understand the basis for the expert's conclusions, the legal team needs to understand how the matter will be explained to the court.

Sometimes the expert will have misunderstood the question that has been posed initially. Sometimes, the legal team may take the view that the expert has given undue weight to some facts and too little weight to others. Sometimes the report will have been phrased in language that is too technical and needs to be explained. In any of these cases, the expert will need to assist the legal team to ensure that the issues are appropriately addressed in such a way that they can be explained to the court.

In addition to the duty to act in a professional manner, the expert witness owes a duty of loyalty to the client. In the 2020 case of *A v B*[27] heard by the High Court of England and Wales, a party to a large international arbitration had retained a firm to provide 'expert services'. A company within the same group became involved in separate but related arbitration, and the firm of experts accepted instructions from another party to that arbitration. The original party applied to the courts for an injunction to restrain the experts from acting in the second arbitration. The High Court took the view that expert witnesses had a 'fiduciary duty of loyalty' to the party instructing them (that is to say, a duty of trust and confidence). They were not entitled to accept instructions that conflicted with that duty.

> If you accept instructions from a client or legal team, your duty is to act with reasonable skill and care, to the best of your professional ability. If you have overlooked matters in your original report, or failed adequately to explain them, it is your duty to correct this, and to answer any relevant questions. You also have a duty of loyalty, not to accept instructions from other parties that might conflict with your duty to the client.

9. To co-operate with the other legal teams when required

> There is no room today in properly conducted litigation for an approach which denies one side access to relevant material which in any event will be available at a later stage of the proceedings. ... Once proceedings have been instituted, [a medical] examination and full access to the Plaintiff's medical records and interviews with his medical advisors are of assistance in enabling the Defendants to form a view as to the amount of damages which the Plaintiff is likely to recover and of any lodgement which they should prudently make in court with their defence. Whether or not liability is a live issue in the case, making such material available to the Defendant at an early stage of the litigation, instead of withholding it until the action itself, when it will have to be produced, can only facilitate the earlier settlement of actions.[28] (*McGrory v Electricity Supply Board*, Supreme Court of Ireland)

Because of the special position of the expert in assembling evidence and explaining technical matters to the court, it is sometimes necessary for an expert or professional witness to co-operate with the legal teams of the other parties to the case.

In general, this will be a matter of asking questions concerning the experts' report after they have been exchanged. Such questions may be asked after agreement between the legal teams, or after an order of the court.

In exceptional circumstances, it will be necessary for, say, the injured party's treating doctor to meet the expert witnesses for the other side, in order that the experts have sufficient access to the primary facts of the case. If an expert has conducted a primary investigation, taking photographs, notes, sketches or tests, it will be necessary for the other legal team to see these in order to meet the case properly.

Such contact will normally only take place after it has been agreed between the parties or directed by the court.

> If you have primary factual information concerning the case, you may be required to disclose this the other legal team by agreement with your own legal team.

10. To co-operate with other experts when required

[I]n every case of this kind there are generally many 'irreducible and stubborn facts' upon which agreement between experts should be possible and in my judgment the expert advisers of the parties, whether legal or scientific are under a special duty to the Court in the preparation of such a case to limit in every possible way the contentious matters of fact to be dealt with at the hearing. That is the duty which exists notwithstanding that it may not always be easy to discharge.[29] (*Graigola v Swansea Corporation*, High Court of England and Wales)

It is only because of their expertise and assumed independence that [experts] are entitled to offer opinion evidence on matters central to the court's determination. If this process functions properly, there should not be wide and unbridgeable gaps between the views of experts. Where there are differences, those should be capable of identification along with the relevant considerations so that the particular issue or issues which require judicial determination should be capable of ready exposition. Ideally, all of this should occur outside a courtroom and well in advance of the trial. It is not merely that the resolution of disputed issues in a trial forum is an expensive and often frustrating process of determination; it is also that the early identification of the real areas in dispute may encourage parties to come to their own resolution which is likely to be more satisfactory to them, and certainly cheaper.[30] (*Emerald Meats Ltd v Minister for Agriculture*, Supreme Court of Ireland)

If two experts with a similar professional background consider the same facts but come to different conclusions there must be a reason for this. If each of them has written a succinct report explaining their methodology and conclusions clearly, it should be possible for the educated reader to identify the primary points of difference without too much difficulty.

It is then the job of the experts to meet and attempt to resolve these differences as far as possible. In some countries, experts are required to prepare a joint report following such a meeting to set out where the differences still lie.

If one or more of the expert witnesses fails to adopt the proper professional approach, there can be a huge cost in both time and money to the parties and to the courts, not to mention the reduced opportunity to settle the case.

Experts who take a partisan approach are in danger of glossing over inconvenient facts and presenting only the theories that appear to suit their client. They may also seek to introduce 'red herrings', turning minor considerations into major issues.

If these matters are not resolved before the trial of the action, an expert could take hours or days in the witness box seeking to elaborate in great detail on matters that are almost irrelevant to the central issue that the expert is supposed to be considering. Given the number of highly-paid personnel in court at any given time, each hour of court time is costly to the parties, and to the court system itself. An expert who seeks to enlarge the issues rather than reduce them can cause incalculable loss.

Furthermore, if the parties to the case have been given widely differing expert advice on a central question, it is less likely that they will be in a position to settle. If they have been led to believe that their case is stronger than it really is, they will be more prepared to let it proceed to trial. Only later will they suffer the consequences.

For this reason, the experts retained by the parties are under an obligation to meet, not as negotiators for the parties who have retained them, but as professionals jointly addressing questions put to them to resolve. They should seek to agree on matters of primary fact, where such facts are not resolved in their respective reports. They should seek to reduce any level of conjecture that has crept into the reports. They should seek to establish what theories or standards are applicable to the question at hand.

And, if it becomes clear that their initial conclusions are no longer tenable, they should be prepared to change their minds.

> If requested by the legal team, or directed by the court, you should:
> - read and comment on the reports of other experts;
> - meet the other experts to discuss the issues between you; and
> - co-operate with the other experts in preparing a joint report on the issues.

11. To communicate any changes of mind on the relevant issues

If, after exchange of reports, an expert witness changes his view on a material matter having read the other side's expert's report or for any other reason, such change of view should be communicated (through legal representatives) to the other side without delay and when appropriate to the Court.[31] (*The Ikarian Reefer*, High Court of England and Wales)

An expert's initial advice is likely to be for the benefit of his client alone. It is on the basis of that advice that the client is likely to decide whether to proceed with his claim, or the terms on which to settle it. The question then arises of the expert's attitude if he subsequently forms the view, or is persuaded by the witness on the other side, that his initial advice was over-optimistic, or that there is some weakness in his client's case which he had not appreciated. His duty to the court is frankly to concede his change of view. The witness of integrity will do so.[32] (*Jones v Kaney*, Supreme Court of the United Kingdom)

Inevitably, there will be times when experts change their view of a case. From the time they were initially retained to provide a report, to the time they are called to give evidence in court, new facts are likely to emerge and they are likely to have to consider the views of the other experts involved in the case. While professionals with integrity will explain such a change of mind to the client, it can give rise to problems for the professionals themselves.

Experts who start out with a bullish view of the wrongdoing of the other party may find over time that their views become more nuanced. Sometimes, they may simply conclude that the initial view was wrong. Where experts do come to a change of mind, this should be communicated first to the instructing legal team.

The duty to communicate a change of mind arises primarily from the obligations of the expert to the court, to tell the truth about the facts and the relevant professional expertise. If the case, or some aspect of it, is no longer tenable, the expert should not attempt to finesse the matter by suggesting that it can still be pursued. The courts are always keen to promote early settlements of cases, and experts should be frank about their assessment.

The duty also arises from the secondary obligation to the expert's own client, to act with reasonable skill and care. Just as the client and legal team will have relied on the expert's assessment in deciding to pursue the case, or part of it, they will need to know as soon as possible if it is necessary to discontinue it, or settle it on less favourable terms. Otherwise, they are likely to expend further funds needlessly.

Experts should also have regard to their own professional integrity. To make a mistake (if one has been made) is unfortunate, but is unlikely to be considered particularly unprofessional. To cover up a mistake may be fraudulent.

Nonetheless, the professionals in question should be aware of the possible consequences. If the change of mind arises from a new or newly-discovered fact, of which experts were unaware, they cannot be faulted. But if they overlooked a significant fact, or failed to address a relevant professional consideration, there is a danger that they could be accused of negligence by their own client, or reported to their professional body.

The consequences of failing to disclose the change of mind are likely to be worse. If the expert persists to the hearing of the case, sticking doggedly to an untenable view, not only will the client lose, but the expert's own professional reputation will be destroyed.

> If your conclusions on a case change at any stage, particularly following receipt of another report, or a meeting with another expert, your duty is to communicate this to your client or legal team. If you take the view that your original conclusion was a mistake on your part (rather than, say, because you were provided with insufficient facts), you should consider whether to notify your own insurer or take independent legal advice.

12. To comply with any directions of the court

During the preparation for a hearing, or during the hearing itself, a professional witness may be subject to directions from a judge concerning the evidence to be given.

The courts have very broad powers to make requirements of parties and witnesses in the preparation of a case, and at the trial. Experts may be directed to answer certain questions concerning a report that has been furnished to the court. They may be directed to attend a meeting with other experts. They could be directed to attend a joint inspection. They could be directed to attend at the site or subject matter of an earlier inspection to reconsider a particular issue.

At the hearing of the trial, the expert evidence is normally heard as part of the evidence of either party. But in the courts of many countries this has been considered unsatisfactory. Rather than asking the experts to give evidence separately, they may be directed to give evidence 'concurrently', in a process sometimes called 'hot-tubbing'. This involves the experts discussing the relevant question in a process a little like a conference chaired by the decision maker.

In rarer cases, experts may be directed by the court to disclose certain material that might normally be considered confidential. While privilege generally attaches to most communication between the expert and the client or legal team, there may be occasions when the court considers that it should be disclosed – perhaps if there is reason to believe that the expert has come under pressure to give evidence to suit the client.

Where the court makes directions of any sort, they are likely to be time-consuming for the expert to comply with. Most busy professionals have difficulty managing their diaries, and it is not uncommon for clients to complain that they have difficulty getting a speedy response from their accountant, architect, doctor or lawyer. The same can sometimes be said when courts make requirements of them.

Where experts are subject to directions from the court (particularly if the directions arise from criticism or implied criticism of their reports) it can be found that the professional in question may be uncooperative or try to prioritise other matters. But the courts of most countries not only expect the professionals to act in a diligent manner, to give the best service to the court, they expect them to give a high priority to court proceedings.

It may sometimes appear to experts that judges have too high a regard for themselves or their work, and that they even abuse their power to direct individuals to appear before them or carry out certain work. Nonetheless, the courts have a public duty to ensure the timely and fair resolution of disputes. One stubborn and uncooperative expert witness can cause delays and expense for the parties to the case, and for all of the lawyers and other professionals involved.

On the criminal side, if a professional witness fails to assist the court in a professional and timely manner, it could result either in a wrongful conviction or the collapse of a trial, often giving rise to public outcry.

So a professional who agrees to play a part in litigation of any sort should be aware, from the outset, of the priority that should attach to such work. In many cases, the work will end with the preparation of a report for one of the parties. There may be professionals who have written numerous reports without ever being called to give evidence or even asked for a follow-up report.

Once instructions are accepted, however, professionals are under an ongoing duty to assist the court to resolve the case, and all reasonable co-operation should be given.

From the time you are instructed in a case, your primary duty is to the court. You may be required to:
- take steps to narrow down the issues in a case;
- answer questions;
- provide documents;
- conduct inspections;
- meet certain persons;
- attend preliminary hearings;
- give evidence in certain ways; or
- be recalled by the court to clarify your evidence.

The court has broad powers to compel parties and witnesses to take certain steps. If you feel that unreasonable demands are being made of you, you should communicate this to the legal team. If you remain unsatisfied with the situation, you might consult your professional body for guidance, or take independent legal advice.

Conclusion

The principle duty of an expert witness is to the decision maker, to tell the truth and to act in a professional manner in giving guidance on the relevant issue. Experts also have duties to their own clients.

If they breach these duties, they need to be broadly aware of what the consequences will be. These consequences will be discussed in Chapter 3.

Notes

1.   See Appendix 3.
2.   *National Justice Compania Naviera SA v Prudential Assurance Company Ltd ('The Ikarian Reefer')* [1995] 1 Lloyd's Rep 455, (8 December 1994) Court of Appeal, Lord Justice Stuart Smith (judgment of the court).
3.   [2000] EWHC Technology 127.
4.   Lord Woolf, Master of the Rolls had produced a report entitled 'Access to Justice' in 1996, which gave rise to these changes.
5.   The updated list of duties is set out in Appendix 3 to this volume.
6.   *Derby & Co Ltd v Weldon* (No.9) 1990 WL 753500 (1990).
7.   'Expert witnesses jailed in London after perjury on "industrial scale"' *The Guardian* (16 June 2017).
8.   *Liverpool Victoria Insurance Company Ltd v Zafar* [2019] EWCA 392 (Civ).
9.   *Whitehouse v Jordan* [1980] UKHL 12 (17 December 1980).
10.   *White Burgess Langille Inman v Abbott and Haliburton Co Ltd* [2015] 2 SCR 182.
11.   *Cala Homes (South) Ltd & Ors v Alfred McAlpine Homes East Ltd* [1995] EWHC 7 (Ch) (06 July 1995).
12.   *The Ikarian Reefer*; but see the qualifying comments made by the Court of Appeal in that case: 'It is evident that in this case the Judge was concerned to confine each expert to his area of expertise; but it is not always possible to do so and where the subject of inquiry is fire, an experienced fire expert, when he is assessing the significance of certain evidence, must be entitled to weigh the probabilities and this may involve making use of the skills of other experts or drawing on his general mechanical or chemical knowledge.' *The Ikarian Reefer* [1994] EWCA Civ J1208-7; [1995] 1 Lloyd's Rep 455 (8 December 1994).
13.   'Fallon in the clear as £10m case collapses: Race-fixing trial abandoned after witness deemed inadequate' *The Guardian* (8 December 2007).
14.   *State Of Himachal Pradesh v Jai Lal* (Supreme Court of India, 13 September 1999), (1999) 7 SCC 280.
15.   *Kennedy v Cordia* [2016] UKSC 6.
16.   *R v Nksatlala* 1960 (3) SA 543 (A) at 546C-D. This case was cited with approval by the post-apartheid South African High Court in *Twine v Naidoo* (38940/14) [2017] ZAGPJHC 288; [2018] 1 All SA 297 (GJ) (16 October 2017).
17.   *Coopers (South Africa) (Pty) Ltd v Deutsche Gesellschaft für Schädlingsbekämpfung mbH* (1976) (3) SA 352.
18.   *Kennedy v Cordia* [2016] UKSC 6.
19.   *Re J (Child Abuse: Expert Evidence)* [1991] FCR 193.
20.   *Fitzpatrick v DPP* [1997] IEHC 180 (High Court, McCracken J, 5 December 1997).
21.   *Jacobson v Sveen*, 2000 ABQB 215.
22.   *Rockwater v Technip France* [2004] EWCA 381. Note: this is a patent case where the term 'skilled in the art' takes on a particular meaning, and the use of the term 'skilled man' should be read in that light.
23.   *Davie v Magistrates of Edinburgh* [1953] SC 34.
24.   [2001] NSWCA 305 (NSW Court of Appeal, 14 September 2001).
25.   *Jones v Kaney* [2011] 2 All ER 671, [2011] 2 AC 398, [2011] UKSC 13, [2011] 2

WLR 823, 135 Con LR 1, [2011] BLR 283, [2011] 14 EG 95.

26   Mrs Justice O'Farrell in *A v B* [2020] EWHC 809 (TCC) (High Court of England and Wales, 3 April 2020).

27   [2020] EWHC 809 (TCC) (3 April 2020).

28   *McGrory v Electricity Supply Board* [2003] IESC 45 (24 July 2003), Keane CJ.

29   *Graigola v Swansea Corporation* [1928] 1 Ch 31.

30   *Emerald Meats Ltd v Minister for Agriculture* [2012] IESC 48.

31   *National Justice Compania Naviera SA v Prudential Assurance Company Ltd; 'The Ikarian Reefer'* [1993] 2 Lloyd's Rep 68.

32   *Jones v Kaney* [2011] 2 All ER 671.

Chapter 3

Enforcement of Experts' Duties

If an expert falls short in relation to any of the duties to the court or to the client, there are a number of consequences that may follow. These may vary from country to country, and court to court, so can only be outlined in a general manner.

Powers of the decision maker to enforce the experts' duties

In most cases, misconduct by expert witnesses will result in penalties for the client rather than the witnesses themselves. The decision maker, whether judge or arbitrator, generally has the following powers available:

Ruling the evidence inadmissible

Where expert witnesses have manifestly not complied with their duties, it is generally open to the court or arbitrator to rule their evidence inadmissible, in part or in total. This means that the evidence, or the relevant part of it, will not even be considered by the court in making its decision.

Placing less weight on the evidence

If one expert has produced a report or given evidence that is less helpful to the court, the logical result is that it will be given less weight. The client is more likely to lose the case, or at least the relevant issue.

Costs

Where a case reaches finality, the usual rule in common law jurisdictions is that the costs 'follow the event', which is to say that the losing party normally pays the costs of the winning party. However, a trial judge generally has broad discretion in awarding costs. If, for example, it was felt that the winning party had used too much court time in attempting to rely on expert evidence that was unsustainable, the relevant portion of the costs could be awarded against that party.

Wasted costs

In exceptional circumstances, the court will take the view that the legal team has acted in an inappropriate manner, irrespective of the instructions given by their clients. The court in those circumstances can make what is known as a 'wasted costs' order, requiring that the lawyers pay the costs themselves. This generally only arises where the legal team has acted in a 'vexatious' manner, bringing cases with no hope of success or deliberately wasting court time.

Costs ordered against the expert witness in person

A 'wasted costs' order may be made in some jurisdictions against an expert witness in person.

In the 2004 English case of *Phillips v Symes*,[1] a consultant psychiatrist had given evidence that a party to the case had, due to a stroke, been unable to manage his own affairs for a period of over 20 years. This flew in the face of overwhelming evidence to the contrary. The expert was warned of a costs order being made against him, but persisted in giving evidence that the court found to be untenable. An application was subsequently made to join him as a party to the case for the purpose of making a 'wasted costs' order against him. Without finally deciding the issue of costs, the court held that, where experts had acted in 'flagrant disregard' of their duties to the court, they could be joined to the case for that purpose.

The power of a court to order an expert witness to pay costs is only rarely likely to arise. The expert should have been warned in advance before such an order is made, and it would only arise if experts had flagrantly wasted court time by their conduct or by giving untenable evidence. But this may vary from country to country.

Public criticism of an expert witness

A rarely-discussed, but widely exercised power of a court is to denounce a person in public. Because most courts hearings are open to the public and the press, and because the proceedings are generally 'privileged' from an action in defamation, a comment by a judge about any person may be reported in the press without consequence.

Furthermore, where a judge delivers a written judgment, it can often include scathing criticism of parties or witnesses. Again, these are protected by privilege.[2]

The consequences for an expert witness could be serious. A search for the expert's name in 'Legal Information Initiatives' (LIIs, such as AUSTLII, BAILII or CANLII), could show up any perceived shortcomings as discussed by the judge. These could result in law firms deciding not to instruct the expert in future cases. Furthermore, comments made by a judge concerning the expert witness during the hearing could be published by the press.

As arbitrations are almost always conducted in private, there is less danger of public embarrassment for expert witnesses.

Proceedings against the expert witness in person

Traditionally, parties, lawyers and witnesses were considered immune from suit in relation to their conduct of court proceedings. The fear was of a multiplicity of actions arising from the original case, where the losing party would seek compensation from the lawyers and witnesses who had acted. In more recent times, courts in a number of countries have concluded that such immunity was not in the public interest.

Professional negligence

Witness immunity was a longstanding principle of English law until a 2011 case called *Jones v Kaney*.[3] This arose from a personal injuries case where a clinical psychologist concluded that the injured party was suffering from a psychiatric disorder. At a later stage, the psychologist signed a joint statement with an expert witness for the other party, concluding that the injured party did not have such a disorder. The case was settled for less than had originally been hoped for, and the injured party proceeded to sue the psychologist. In a controversial decision, the UK Supreme Court decided, by a majority, that there was no longer immunity from suit for expert witnesses. This approach has found some favour in New Zealand[4] and Canada.[5]

Although there is no uniformity concerning the immunity from suit, it would be foolhardy for any expert witness to assume that any clear breach of duty that causes loss to the client would not give rise to some remedy.

Disciplinary measures

Most professions have some measure of self-regulation, seeking to uphold standards and to discipline those members of the profession who fail to meet them.

As with professional negligence actions, it was traditionally considered that expert witnesses were immune from professional discipline in respect of their conduct in court. In the UK, this view was set aside in the 2006 case of *General Medical Council v Meadows*,[6] which arose from the high-profile case of *R v Clark*.[7] The Court of Appeal of England and Wales unanimously rejected the idea that witness immunity extended to 'fitness to practice' proceedings.

Disciplinary measures are routinely brought against professionals in some jurisdictions arising from their conduct in court actions. For example, in a 2019 Australian case, a clinical psychologist was banned by his professional body from acting as an expert witness, and fined AUS\$20,000, for his conduct in a family law case. His 'Single Expert Witness Report' had attributed 'traits of psychopathy' to a father, and suggested that his child needed protection from him. He subsequently admitted that there had been insufficient data or clinical evidence for such findings.[8]

Any immunity for expert witnesses from disciplinary measures seems harder to justify than immunity from a professional negligence suit. If experts in any jurisdiction bring their profession into disrepute, it is only reasonable to expect their professional colleagues to take appropriate action.

Criminal penalties against expert witnesses

In addition to the 'civil' penalties discussed above, experts are subject to the criminal law in the same way as any other witness. If they knowingly mislead the court from the witness box, or on affidavit, they can expect to face a charge of perjury. If they act in 'contempt of court', either by refusing to follow direction of the court, or by seeking to prejudice a trial, they are liable to face prosecution.

Most court actions have serious consequences for the parties involved. If you breach any of the duties owed to the court or your clients, by acting in an unprofessional manner or misleading the court, there may be consequences for you. If you have concerns in this regard, consult your professional body or your insurer, or take independent legal advice.

Conclusion

Professionals are less likely to face any of the penalties set out in this chapter if they understand the duties set out in Chapter 2. They will also be protected if they ask certain questions before they accept instructions. These are outlined in the next chapter.

Notes

1   [2004] EWHC 2330.
2   Criticism deterring medical specialists from being expert witnesses' by Monidiper Fouzda, in the *Law Society Gazette*, 29 November 2019.
3   [2011] UKSC 13.
4   *EBR Holdings Limited (in liquidation) v McLaren Guise Associates Limited* [2016] NZCA 622.
5   *Halpern v Morris* (2016) ONSC 7855 (CanLII).
6   [2006] EWHC 146.
7   [2003] EWCA Crim 1020.
8   *Psychology Board of Australia and Menaglio* [2018] VR 47.

Chapter 4

Accepting Instructions

When a professional is approached by a legal team to provide a court report, or to act as an expert witness, some caution is required before accepting instructions. The issue at first may appear to be a simple one, one that can be addressed in a short court report. But, at the beginning of any case it is rarely possible to be sure how it will progress. It may be that the court report will become controversial, requiring the involvement of other experts, and the writer could face cross-examination on the report at a later stage.

This chapter sets out a number of steps that a professional should take prior to accepting instructions.

Clarifying the issues

'A well defined problem is already half solved.' Charles Kettering

> Expert evidence must be confined to the live issues between the parties. ... The expert should not be left to define for himself the questions he has to answer from reading lengthy pleadings (or affidavits in this case). Questions for the expert should preferably be framed as 'yes' or 'no' or 'multiple choice' questions.[1] (*Fo Shan Shi Shun De Qu Consonancy Investment Co Ltd v Yat Kit Jong*, High Court of Hong Kong SAR)

The reason that an expert or professional witness is retained in a case is to assist the court to determine an issue outside the decision maker's expertise. But it is not uncommon for a legal team to ask a professional to provide a report without setting out what specific issue needs to be addressed. While this is primarily a matter for the legal team, experts should ensure that they too understand the question to be addressed.

Civil litigation

In civil litigation generally the questions are determined on the 'balance of probability'. In most cases alleging tort or breach of contract, there are four broad questions to address:

1. Whether there was wrongdoing by the defendant (a tort or breach of contract);
2. What injury, loss or damage was suffered by the claimant;
3. Whether (and to what extent) the wrongdoing caused the injury, loss or damage;
4. What remedy the decision maker should order, in terms of compensation or (for example) injunctive relief.

It will be observed that the issues of wrongdoing and causation can generally be framed as 'yes' or 'no' questions. The issues of injury and compensation are questions that may require descriptive and quantitative answers.

In complex cases such as medical negligence actions, it is possible that different experts will be required to address all four broad questions. While the issues of wrongdoing, injury and causation will probably require medical experts, the issue of remedy may require actuaries or occupational therapists (where, for example, a claimant sustained a permanent disability as a result of the alleged negligence).

Other civil cases may require more specific questions to be addressed. For example, in probate cases, the question often arises as to whether the testator was of sound mind when they executed their will. Because wills are often executed late in the testator's life, symptoms of cognitive impairment may already have become apparent, and most legal systems ask that particular questions are addressed in relation to whether the testator was of sound mind. If the psychiatric evidence addresses only the general issue of soundness of mind, without addressing the specific legal question, it may not be sufficient to assist the decision maker.

Criminal litigation

In criminal cases, to secure a conviction, most questions need to proved 'beyond a reasonable doubt', which is a higher standard of proof than in civil litigation.

The primary questions to be answered in these cases will be set out in the charges against the accused person. But many other questions will arise from these. DNA evidence or fingerprint evidence may be adduced to establish whether the accused was at the scene of the alleged offence. Forensic evidence may be relied upon to establish, for example, whether the accused handled explosives. Evidence from medical professionals may be introduced to establish whether the injuries to the alleged victim were consistent with the allegations made against the accused.

Because of the risks of a wrongful conviction, the professionals are required to address these questions in an impartial manner. They are also expected not to exceed the limits of the question to be asked. For example, where a fingerprint expert is asked to give evidence, the question will relate to whether the fingerprint at the scene of an alleged crime matches that of the accused person. The expert should answer the question, together with the level of certainty that can be given. They should not then proceed to conclude: 'Therefore, I have little doubt that the accused was at the scene of the offence.' This would be a matter for the judge or jury who has considered the evidence.

General

If the question to be addressed is not well-framed at the outset, there is a danger that the expert will write a general report that does not consider the relevant issues, or that there will be excessive focus on matters that are not central to the determination of the court.

Before you accept instructions, ensure that the question to be addressed is properly set out. If you have any doubts, ask the instructing legal team for clarification.

Ensuring that the professional is appropriately qualified

Once the experts have ensured that the question is properly framed, they should ensure that they are appropriately qualified to answer it. If the question is simply outside their area of expertise, they should not accept the instructions.

Level of expertise is also to be considered. In every field of expertise, there are different levels of specialisation. In a small case concerning a minor injury, it may be appropriate to retain a general practitioner to provide a report. But where the injuries are severe, permanent or complex, a specialist would almost certainly be required. Ultimately, it is a matter for the client and legal team to decide on which expert to retain, based on their own knowledge of the case; however, it would unlikely to assist the case if a professional with a general knowledge of the area were to act as an expert witness, only to find that the other side had retained a team of highly specialised experts.

So a certain amount of humility would be advisable for any professional who considers whether to accept instructions. Better to allow another person to be retained than for the client to be faced down by a more specialised or experienced expert, or – as is also quite likely – for the professionals' reputation to be damaged by publicly facing questions they are not qualified to answer.

> Before accepting instructions, consider whether you are the appropriate professional to address the question. If it is clearly outside your specialisation, you should not accept instructions. If you have doubts, discuss them with the legal team.

Disclosing potential conflicts of interest

> Can an expert give opinion evidence for a friend who is sued on a matter within the expert's area of expertise? I expect the answer is generally 'yes' but the defendant who relies on the expert evidence of a friend runs the risk the evidence may be given little or no weight, particularly where, as in this case, the expert opinion on medical practise includes a testimonial about what a good doctor the Defendant is.[2] (*MacWilliams v Connor*, Supreme Court of Prince Edward Island)

Ideally, every witness would be entirely unbiased and give the unvarnished truth to the decision maker. In reality, many ordinary witnesses have a connection to one of the parties, and may be reluctant to be as frank as they might otherwise be. In particular, where a family member or an employee is called to give evidence, it may be difficult for that person to say damaging things about their loved one or boss.

Many professionals are asked to provide reports or called to give evidence because of their connection with one of the parties. A treating doctor may be required to provide a report about a patient. Health and safety supervisors may be required to provide a report about an accident they have investigated at a construction site, or at a shopping centre. This is generally primary factual evidence and the professional in question will be expected to tell the truth.

Issues of bias become more difficult when it comes to 'opinion evidence'. If the conclusion of an expert is central to the determination of the question, it is important that the expert is independent of the instructing client and that there is no perception of bias.

Where there is a clear conflict of interest, it should be apparent to experts that they should not give evidence in the case. For example, a medical expert should not give opinion evidence as to whether a close colleague was negligent in the treatment of a patient.

In other cases, the damage may arise not from any actual conflict of interest, but from the perception of it. For example, if an engineer were to give evidence in a case involving a manufacturing company, it might be seen to damage the case if it transpired that they had previously worked for a related company. Similarly, it might look questionable if an expert turned out to have a shareholding in a company for which they were acting, either in their own name or as part of a pension portfolio. If the expert works in an academic institution, it may be that their research work has been sponsored by a company that is party to the case. If these potential conflicts are disclosed to the legal team at the outset, they can decide whether they are likely to damage the testimony of the expert. If they do decide to retain the expert, and the potential conflicts are disclosed to the other parties, it will be considerably less damaging than if the conflict is discovered at a later date and raised in cross-examination.

Ultimately, the issue to be determined is whether the decision maker can rely on the evidence of the professional in question. If the professional is appropriately qualified, and addresses the question in a thorough manner, it is unlikely that a distant or past connection with one of the parties will undermine their evidence. What would damage it is if the connection were not disclosed, and the decision maker decided to give the evidence less weight as a consequence.

> If you have a direct family or financial connection with one of the parties, you should not give opinion evidence on a question central to the determination of the case. If you have a more remote or past connection with one of the parties, you should disclose this to the legal team before you accept instructions. It will then be a matter for them to decide whether to continue to instruct you. If a connection emerges after accepting instructions that you were previously unaware of, you should disclose this as soon as possible.

Matters concerning the professional's reputation

The UK Supreme Court case of *McBride v Scottish Police Authority* concerned an experienced fingerprint officer employed by the Scottish Criminal Records Office.[3] In 1997 she had been involved in a high-profile murder trial where the conviction was later set aside arising from issues concerning the fingerprint evidence. This resulted in questions concerning all fingerprint evidence provided by the office. Although the expert in question was cleared of wrongdoing in a subsequent investigation and returned to employment, it was decided that she could not return to court-going duties. There was a fear that if she were called as a witness by the prosecution in future cases, defence counsel would focus their cross-examination on the earlier controversy.

In large-value cases, it has long been the practice of the parties to engage in detailed research concerning the experts retained by the other parties. Now that personal histories are widely available through online research, it would be difficult for a professional to conceal any matters that could affect their reputation.

Nobody likes to be reminded of past mistakes. However, if professionals have been involved in controversial matters that might be used to discredit their testimony, it would be better – from the client's point of view – that this be known at the outset.

If you have been involved in controversial matters in the past that might be used to discredit your testimony, it would be advisable to notify the instructing legal team. It will be a matter for them to decide whether it is sufficiently damaging to retain you. If you would prefer not to discuss the matter, it might be safer simply to refuse to accept instructions, rather than allow it to be raised at a later date.

Fee quotation

At the outset of any case it can be difficult to know how much work the expert will be required to do. The case may settle or be discontinued after the first report is written. Or the expert may be required to do a considerable amount of other work, including:

- writing follow-up reports;
- considering reports from other experts;
- meeting other experts;
- consulting with the client, other witnesses and the legal team;
- attending mediation;
- giving evidence in court or arbitration.

In most civil cases, in most court systems and arbitrations, the costs 'follow the event', meaning that the losing party has to pay the costs of the winning party. Disputes about these costs can rumble on long after the litigation itself has completed. While a fee quotation will not necessarily determine the costs to be awarded in respect of the professional in question, it will be extremely helpful to the client in seeking to recover the costs.

For this reason, before accepting instructions, the expert would be well-advised to furnish the legal team with a detailed schedule of fees, to include (where relevant):

- the cost of on-site visits;
- the cost of preparing an expert report;
- costs of any further research or reports required;
- the cost of attending meetings or consultations;
- any costs associated with additional staff, such as junior colleagues or administrative staff;
- the daily costs of attending mediation, arbitration or other alternative dispute resolution;
- any 'stand-by' costs that might arise for being available to attend court at short notice if required, or being available to answer telephone queries during mediations or settlement meetings;
- any costs of third-party consultants, such as research laboratories conducting analysis of samples;
- costs of equipment hire or purchase; and
- costs of travel, meals and accommodation.

Each profession will have its own likely expenses, so the quotation should provide as much relevant detail as necessary. The more specific the quotation is at the outset, the harder it will be for the client or the other parties to dispute it at a later date. The legal team may require quotations on specific items, or in a particular form, so the expert should enquire about them at the outset.

If the professional is retained following the approval of the quotation, it is advisable that a record is kept of all work done as part of the retainer.

Caution should be adopted by a professional who accepts a fee that might be considered inordinately high, as it could give rise to the perception that it led to a conclusion that was more favourable to the client. Such a perception arose in the case of a barrister who was prosecuted in the 2014 Welsh case of *R v Evans*.[4] A company owned open-cast mines, held subject to a covenant requiring them to restore the lands when mining ceased. A scheme was devised whereby the freehold interest in the land would be transferred by the mining company to a company based in the British Virgin Islands (BVI), so that the mining company would not be subject to the massively expensive restoration obligations. A Queen's Counsel (senior barrister) was retained to give an opinion on whether the mining company would remain liable under the covenants. In his original opinion, he concluded that they would remain liable. Later, and after an up-front fee of £250,000 was paid to him, he produced a second opinion, concluding that the mining company would have no restoration obligations, as they would be assumed by the company in the BVI.

When the opinion, and the fee paid for it, came to the attention of the Serious Fraud Office, they took the view that this had not been a valid legal opinion. The barrister (amongst others involved in the scheme) was charged with 'conspiracy to defraud'. As recounted by Mr Justice Hinckinbottom in the judgment:

> The Crown relies upon a statement from [the barrister's] clerk, upon being told of the size of the fee for the second opinion negotiated by [the barrister] personally: 'Fuck me, that's a serious amount of money'. That, it is said, is the clearest evidence that the fee was much more than anything that could be described as commercial,[5]

An application was made by the accused persons to have the charge dismissed, on the grounds that the evidence against them was not sufficient for them to be properly convicted. A number of members of the chancery bar made submissions before the court concerning the issues in the opinion. The court was satisfied that the prosecution had overstepped the mark in seeking to prosecute for 'conspiracy to defraud'. The object of the alleged conspiracy and the means by which it were to be achieved had both been lawful, and the charge was dismissed.

Nonetheless, this is a cautionary tale for any expert who is paid an extremely high fee for a court report, or to give evidence. If the fee were disclosed to the other parties, or to the court, it could give rise to the perception that the expert's view was not entirely objective. It might, accordingly, be given less weight.

Conversely, a professional witness who accepts a fee that is notably lower than the norm might be perceived to have other reasons to want to assist the client.

In some types of case, particularly personal injuries cases, it is common for the lawyers and experts to accept instructions on a 'no win, no fee' basis. (Also known as 'conditional fee arrangements' or 'success fee agreements'. In Ireland, a horse-breeding analogy is adopted, and the term 'no foal, no fee' is preferred.[6])

In England and Wales, it has been held that any such arrangement should be disclosed to the court, in the 2002 case of R *(Factortame) v Secretary of State for Transport*:

> Where an expert has an interest of one kind or another in the outcome of the case, this fact should be made known to the court as soon as possible. The question of whether the proposed expert should be permitted to give evidence should then be determined in the course of case management.[7]

This statement has been approved by the courts of New Zealand[8] and Ireland.[9]

Such an arrangement carries with it an obvious conflict of interest, in that the professionals involved are unlikely to be paid anything if the injured party loses the case. In some countries — notably the United Kingdom — attempts have been made to limit such arrangements. However, for many people of limited means, it would be difficult to fund litigation if such arrangements were prohibited altogether. If professionals were not to be able to accept 'no win, no fee' instructions, it would be necessary to have a system of civil legal aid, or 'after the event' insurance, for the injured parties to vindicate their rights.

Before accepting instructions on a 'no win, no fee' basis, experts should ask the legal team to clarify the rules currently in place.

Before you accept instructions, provide the legal team with a detailed quotation for any work you may be required to do on the case. If you are being asked to accept work on a 'no win, no fee' basis, ensure that this is in accordance with the rules currently in place, and that any disclosure rules are complied with.

Insurance

Before accepting instructions to act as a professional or expert witness for a fee, it would be advisable for professionals to check that their professional indemnity insurance policy covers such work. As discussed in the previous chapter, immunity from suit concerning expert evidence is under threat in a number of common law countries. If there is any limit on such cover, this should be brought to the attention of the client or legal team.

Conclusion

Before a professional accepts instructions in a particular action it is important that the client and legal team are satisfied that the right person is being retained, and that any risk of later regret is minimised. By asking the right questions at the outset, professionals can make sure that they do not accept instructions in a matter for which they are not qualified, or where there is an unacceptable connection with one of the parties.

Once the professional has accepted instructions, it will be necessary to conduct factual investigations concerning the case, as will be discussed in the next chapter.

Notes

1   *Fo Shan Shi Shun De Qu Consonancy Investment Co Ltd v Yat Kit Jong* [2017] HKEC 557.

2   *MacWilliams v Connors* (2014) PESC 12 (Supreme Court of Prince Edward Island, Taylor J, 11 April 2014).

3   [2016] UKSC 27.

4   [2014] EW Misc 5 (CrownC) (Crown Court, Mr Justice Hinckinbottom, 18 February 2014).

5   Oddly, the sentence in the published judgment ends with a comma, suggesting that the judge originally intended to add something else, but changed his mind.

6   See, for example: *Used Car Importers of Ireland Ltd v Minister for Finance* [2014] IEHC 256 (27 February 2014).

7   [2002] EWCA Civ 932 (3 July 2002).

8   *Snowdon v Radio New Zealand Limited* [2014] NZEmpC 45 (1 April 2014).

9   *O'Leary v Mercy University Hospital Cork Ltd* [2019] IESC 48 (31 May 2019).

Chapter 5

Factual Investigations

General considerations

When conducting factual investigations in preparation for a court report, there are a few matters the professional witness should bear in mind.

Role of the expert

The role of the expert or professional witness is to assist the court, not to advance an explanation that would help the client win the case. Therefore, any investigation should consider any alternative explanations that might assist the other parties to the case, in order to test their validity. If two expert witnesses appear in court, each with different explanations or theories but without evaluating the other theory, the court will probably find it difficult to choose between them. More weight will be given to the testimony of experts who are able not only to give their own conclusions, but to explain why they have discounted other explanations.

Rival investigations

In many cases, more than one expert will investigate the same subject matter. Even if there is a 'single joint expert' retained to conduct investigations, it is possible that the same materials will be looked at by an expert from another discipline, or that one of the parties will not be happy with the report and seek to retain a further expert. If there is a factual contradiction between two experts in the case, it is likely (although not guaranteed) that the court will place more reliance on the expert who has conducted the more thorough investigation. This does not mean that the expert should spend several days conducting a site inspection that would otherwise take a couple of hours. But more time spent double-checking measurements, or examining other materials, will make the report more reliable, and could lead to a considerable saving in court time.

The adversarial system

In an adversarial system, the role of cross-examining counsel is to pick holes in the evidence given by the other party. Any ambiguity is likely to be seized upon to suggest that the conclusions in the report are unreliable. Any omissions in the investigation could be emphasised to suggest that the expert was not considering the alternative explanations in the case. Experts who can show that they conducted a methodical and thorough investigation are less likely to be embarrassed in the witness box. A material fact that can be corroborated by more than one source is less likely to be questioned.

Requirement of clarity

When conducting the investigation, the expert should bear in mind that the findings will need to be presented to laypersons in the report, and possibly in court. This does not mean that the expert should omit any complexity in the report. It means that the complexity needs to be properly explained. It can be of assistance to show some context, rather than focusing exclusively on the finer detail of the issue.

For all of the above reasons, prior to conducting an investigation, the expert should consider making a plan in advance, with, for example, a checklist of the materials to be examined or photographed. This can also give rise to a more efficient use of the expert's time during the inspection.

For example, architects or engineers who have been asked to examine a defective building could find that there are several defects to examine or explain. If attending with an assistant or two, they could ask their colleagues to measure and photograph the exterior of the building and the individual rooms, while the experts focus on the damage complained of.

In the 2003 English case of *R v Clark*,[1] a murder trial arising from two apparent 'cot deaths' in one family, evidence gathered by a pathologist was withheld from the jury. The Court of Appeal was critical of the conduct of the pathologist in question, and set out in some detail what was expected of a pathologist in a homicide case. This included the information that should be obtained prior to the inspection of the deceased's body, and the examination of all parts of the body – including those without apparent abnormalities. The court went on to say:

> Having reached his conclusions, the pathologist will then prepare a report. That report should detail the information he received in advance of the examination, all the investigations that he has made either personally or by submission to a laboratory for report, his conclusions and an explanation for those conclusions. Where features out of the ordinary are found and the pathologist concludes that they are not relevant, he should explain why he discounts the finding. Thus by way of extreme example, a pathologist examining a man with a shot wound to the head might discover that he had a severe heart condition that could have killed him at any moment. He might nonetheless conclude that the shot wound was such that it would have killed instantaneously any person, however healthy, and that the heart condition can, therefore, have played no part. In such circumstances the clear duty of the pathologist would be to record the heart condition in his report but to explain that since death would have been instantaneous and since the victim was clearly alive when shot, his conclusion was that the heart condition played no part in the death.

While this judgment was directed at pathologists, a similarly thorough approach is recommended for the investigation of crane accidents in a paper from 2017:

> Collecting and reviewing the background information is important in the investigation of crane accidents. Interviewing witnesses provides useful information about the accident(s). Careful and early site survey is critical in collecting important original evidences and guiding subsequent investigation. Laboratory analysis may be needed for further understanding the microscopic features of the failure and providing more physical evidences. Logical thinking in analysing all available data and findings paves the way to draw solid conclusions with sufficient supporting evidences. Structural stress analysis and simulation may be carried out when necessary.

Forensic investigation on crane accidents is accomplished by integrating these processes.[2]

Irrespective of the discipline involved, a thorough and methodical approach to factual investigation is more likely to assist the court to reach the correct result. The reliability of such an investigation will, of course, depend on the records kept by the expert.

Records of investigations

Where expert evidence refers to photographs, plans, calculations, analyses, measurements, survey reports or other similar documents, these must be provided to the opposite party at the same time as the exchange of reports.[3] (*The Ikarian Reefer*, High Court of England and Wales)

A witness may know a particular fact to be true, but if it cannot be corroborated or verified, it will be open to question. At the outset of any investigation, the professional should have some idea of which facts are likely to be questioned, and ensure that careful records are kept of verifiable facts.

Photographs, recordings and videos

When conducting investigations, it is useful for experts to take photographs to include in the report, to illustrate any facts recorded or conclusions reached.

In an era of digital photography anybody conducting a survey or inspection could in theory take thousands of photographs. Bearing in mind the considerations set out above, the expert should at least consider the following:

Context photographs

As well as taking a photograph of the relevant damage, wider shots should be taken of the surrounding context. For example, if there is a wound to a forearm, it may not be clear from the photograph of the wound itself how large or small it is. Another photograph of the whole forearm, including the hand and elbow, will make it clear to any judge or jury how large the wound was at the time of the inspection.

Photographs relevant to other theories

If experts focus entirely on the damage and their own explanation for it the other experts or the cross-examining counsel may seek to suggest that there were other factors that were not considered. For example, if there is damp in a new building it could arise from condensation, ingress of rain or wind, or from a leaking pipe. An expert who ascribes it all to one cause may face a suggestion that it was caused or contributed to by one of the other factors. By inspecting and reporting on the other possible causes, the expert will be better protected from such allegations.

For some investigations, it may be appropriate to make videos or audio recordings. Where the expert takes numerous photographs, or makes recordings of this sort, the safest course of action is to ensure that they are properly stored and made available to the other parties, even if they are not included in the expert's report.

Measurements

'One accurate measurement is worth a thousand expert opinions.' Rear admiral Grace Hopper, computer scientist (1906–1992).

Experts who carry out reliable measurements will not only be harder for cross-examining counsel to undermine, but their reports will seem more authoritative.

Almost anything can be measured in some way. While physical items can be measured in terms of length, weight, area or volume, other more specialised issues can be measured in other ways. If employees of a manufacturing plant are complaining of hearing loss, the noise of the machinery can be measured in decibels. The slipperiness of floors in 'slip and fall' cases can be measured in terms of the 'coefficient of friction'. Where a person is suspected of having reduced cognitive impairment, medical professionals typically use a test called the 'Mini Mental State Examination' – a series of 30 questions that demonstrates the ability of the subject to use language, to recall names or events and to follow commands.

An expert should seek to measure not only the matters relevant to their own theory of the case (or the one their client is seeking to advance), but also the matters relevant to other theories or likely theories.

Where appropriate, the expert should use measurements in context, to assist in presenting the information to the court. It is one matter to say that an area of damp on a wall of a dwelling house measures one metre by two metres. It is another to say that the area of damp was on the wall of a room measuring just three metres by four metres, especially if the measurements are placed beside the relevant photograph in the report.

When taking multiple measurements in the course of an inspection, the danger of making a mistake can arise, or of incorrectly recording one measurement. It could be good practice to have a system of double-checking key measurements, especially if assisted in the inspection by a colleague.

The expert who fails to take adequate measurements is exposed not only to answering difficult questions, but possibly to allegations of failure to conduct a proper inspection.

Drawings or sketches

Some materials are difficult to photograph because of their complexity. Engines and bodily organs can both be difficult for a layperson to look at and understand. For this reason, many professionals like to make sketches to simplify the problem and their explanation for it.

Sketches can also be useful for the reader of a report. Measurements of buildings will be easier to understand if placed on sketch maps or plans, rather than set out in tables. Medical reports sometimes include printed outlines of a human body, so that the professional can sketch the injury onto the outline in a manner that the reader will readily understand.

If sketches are made in suboptimal conditions (wet weather, or oily workplaces), it may be necessary to re-draw them for inclusion in a final report. It is best practice to retain the originals for inspection by the other experts or their instructing legal team.

Samples

Depending on the type of inspection, it may be necessary to take samples for analysis, or to show to the court. Each profession will have its own standards for the taking of such samples, and for their storage (especially if the sample taken is of a type that is likely to deteriorate over time).

If samples are sent to a third-party laboratory for analysis, the 'chain of control' should be recorded and retained to reduce the chance for another party to suggest that they might have been tampered with.

Notes

If a report is written days or even weeks after the date of the inspection, there is a real danger that the cross-examiner will suggest that the writer's memory was faulty, or that certain details were not properly recalled. It is therefore advisable to take a good contemporaneous note of the key issues concerning the investigation.

Depending on the inspection being conducted, the following matters should be recorded:

The date and time of the inspection

The inspection may take place months or even years after the events giving rise to the case. The expert will need to assess whether any lapse in time affects their ability to carry out a reliable inspection.

The conditions of the inspection

A road traffic accident might have taken place at dusk on a wet day, but the inspection might take place at midday on a sunny day. A workplace accident might have taken place while loud machinery was operating in a room crowded with employees, but the inspection could take place while the machinery was silent, and with only a few people around. The expert will need to take such matters into account when writing the report and presenting the evidence.

The personnel present

If the expert is accompanied by the injured party, or a member of the legal team, when conducting the inspection this should be recorded. In most cases, this should not affect the reliability of the inspection, but the failure to record their presence might be seen to undermine it if an account of their presence emerged at a later stage.

Similarly, the expert might be accompanied by junior colleagues, or even work experience students, who could assist in taking measurements or photographs. It is unlikely that other parties would make an issue of their presence if it were recorded. However, if some of the measurements were found to be questionable, and the expert had failed to record the involvement of other personnel, it might be suggested that something was being concealed.

Descriptions of relevant material

If the expert was to take extensive photographs, with a view to writing up the report at a later date, there is a danger that the photographs – being two-dimensional – might not tell the viewer as much as the expert would hope. Another expert, or a cross-examiner, might suggest that the photograph was not consistent with the description in the report.

However, if the expert writes a contemporaneous description of the materials examined this should corroborate the photographs, and should render the description in the report more reliable.

Furthermore, a visual image cannot convey to the reader of the report the reaction of the other four senses, particularly smell, sound or touch.

Interviews with clients and witnesses

Where the expert interviews clients or witnesses concerning matters relevant to the case, it is important to remember that this is generally hearsay information. It is likely that the factual information from these parties will need to be given separately in court.

There is a likelihood in some cases that inconsistencies will emerge between the account given by the witness to the expert and the account given in court, so the expert will need to keep a careful note of what they have been told during such interviews. If the witness told the expert something different from what was said in court, this would be outside the control of the expert. On the other hand, if it were to transpire that the expert had taken an incorrect note, this could be used to undermine other aspects of the expert's testimony.

The contemporaneous notes will often have to made available to other experts and legal teams. If the report either contains material not included in the notes, or omits significant material that is in the notes, it is likely to cast doubt on the reliability of the report.

Documents consulted

Depending on the type of inspection, the expert may be required to read extensive documentation. A case can sometimes turn on a note that was written on a single page. It can, however, become unclear which documents were seen by which experts or parties.

In modern 'white collar' criminal investigations, there can be thousands of documents that could potentially be relevant, and it may be necessary for other personnel to select the ones that appear to be most relevant.

If experts are asked to consider a large amount of documentation, they should ensure that there is a record of which documents have been received. If a material entry appears to have been overlooked, it may be through inadvertence on the part of the expert, or because they never received the document in question.

Experts should also record whether they inspected originals or copies. There could, for example, be notes in pencil on the originals, or on the reverse side of some pages that were not visible on the copies.

Conclusion

When conducting an investigation, experts need to ensure that they will be in a position to write a reliable report. This means a report that has considered all of the relevant factual material, and all of the issues that have been raised in the court proceedings.

If experts can show the court that their investigation has been thorough, they are more likely to have their report accepted. They are also less likely to be embarrassed in cross-examination.

The failure to carry out a proper investigation can fatally undermine an expert's report and evidence. This was illustrated in the 2015 English case of *Van Oord UK Ltd & Anor v Allseas UK Ltd*,[4] a claim arising from the laying of a gas pipeline. A quantity surveyor was retained by the claimant, and the judge found no less than twelve reasons for criticising his report and evidence, including: that he had accepted the pleaded claims at face value, without checking underlying documents; that he had only read the witness statements prepared on behalf of his own clients, without reading the witness statements prepared by the other party; that, even though the shortcomings had been pointed out in the report by the quantity surveyor for the other party, he was caught out on the same issues in cross-examination; he had appended documents to his own report that he had not read; and he had failed to cross-check any of the figures in his report. The judge concluded that his evidence had been 'entirely worthless'.

It is therefore crucial that expert witnesses consider the facts of the case in proper detail, to ensure that they are reliable. They also need to apply the appropriate professional standards, as will be discussed in the next chapter.

Notes

1   [2003] EWCA Crim 1020.
2   'Forensic investigation on crane accidents' by George Y H Yu in *International Journal of Forensic Engineering*, vol 3, no 4 (2017).
3   *National Justice Compania Naviera SA v Prudential Assurance Company Ltd; 'The Ikarian Reefer'* [1993] 2 Lloyd's Rep 68
4   [2015] EWHC 3074 (TCC) (12 November 2015).

Chapter 6

Conducting Professional Research

[T]he opinion of an expert requires demonstration or examination of the scientific or other intellectual basis of the conclusions reached: that is, the expert's evidence must explain how the field of 'specialised knowledge' in which the witness is expert by reason of 'training, study or experience', and on which the opinion is based, applies to the facts assumed or observed so as to produce the opinion propounded. If all these matters are not made explicit, it is not possible to be sure whether the opinion is based wholly or substantially on the expert's specialised knowledge. If the court cannot be sure of that, the evidence is strictly speaking not admissible, and, so far as it is admissible, of diminished weight.[1] (*Makita (Australia) Pty Ltd v Sprowles*, Court of Appeal of New South Wales)

General considerations

In the ordinary course of their work, many professionals do not refer their clients to textbooks or professional literature. When dentists are explaining to patients about how to treat a tooth, the patients would not expect them to open a book to back up their advice. Similarly, when advice is being sought from accountants or architects, the clients would not normally ask them to explain their expertise. It is taken for granted.

An exception might arise where the client has sought a 'second opinion' and needs to decide between conflicting professional advice. The professionals might be asked to back up their advice with the appropriate literature.

The legal profession is a little different from other professions in this regard. Generally, where a lawyer provides an opinion for a client, it is necessary to provide authority for the opinion either in legislation or case law.

So, when professionals are asked to provide advice to the court, and the other side has retained professionals giving conflicting advice, the judge (who is normally a lawyer) would reasonably expect each side's professionals to provide authorities for their respective opinions. Otherwise, how is the court to decide between two eminent experts whose experience is contradictory on a very important issue?

The experts should not be relying on their own professional experience when reaching such an opinion. Their role is not to give a personal opinion but a professional one, grounded in the collective expertise of their profession. It is not asking much of an expert witness, prior to submitting a report—or entering the witness box—to consult the literature on the subject so that the decision maker can be satisfied that the opinion is a reliable one.

The court should never decide a case based on mere conjecture, and the unsupported opinion of an expert witness is in danger of amounting to little more than that. It is the job of the expert to inform the court of the appropriate professional standard so that the court can make its own objective decision on the issue in question. Where experts try to give evidence based solely on their own experience, the courts can be scathing, as can be seen from the following two cases.

In an Irish case in 2020, *Kellett v RCL Cruises Ltd*,[2] a holidaymaker had sued the organiser of a cruise to the Caribbean for injuries she had suffered. When on the island of St Maarten (a territory belonging to the Netherlands), she went on an excursion called a 'White Knuckle Jet Boat Thrill Ride', during which she was lifted from her seat and then thrown back against the gunwale of the boat, fracturing her arm near the elbow. A consultant forensic engineer gave evidence for the injured party suggesting that the organisers had been negligent in a number of ways, including: (i) failure to fit seatbelts; (ii) failure to place a side bar along the side of the boat; and (iii) failure to place padding along the gunwale.

No engineering evidence was given by the defendants. At trial, the High Court dismissed the case, as the engineer had not given any evidence as to the regulations governing such boat trips in either Ireland or St Maarten. An appeal to the Court of Appeal was dismissed unanimously. One of the appeal judges noted:

> The appellant's engineer gave no evidence of any relevant standards or regulations that might have applied to the activity in question in St. Maarten. Although he offered the view that items (i) to (iii) above should, in his opinion, have been provided, he was unable to offer any evidence of such features in any similar craft anywhere with the exception that he had once been on a boat on the Thames which had a side rail.

In a 2016 case from New Zealand,[3] a loss adjustor purported to give expert evidence in a claim against an insurance company arising from damage to a building after a series of earthquakes. Not only was the loss adjustor's position compromised (in that his company had a financial interest in the outcome of the case) but the methodology he adopted did not refer to the relevant professional standards or literature. He relied only on his own 'training and experience'. The case was dismissed by the trial judge and appealed to the Court of Appeal. Here the appeal was also dismissed, the judges saying:

> We have noted that [the witness] cited no professional literature or other material to verify his 'elemental' methodology. He did not suggest that there was anything novel about it. He relied rather on his long experience as a loss adjuster in the United States and explained that he was trained in his methodology when working in the insurance industry. That being so, in our opinion he ought to have been able to point readily to material showing that the methodology was orthodox. The absence of any such evidence is a strong indicator that the methodology lacks reliability.

They concluded: 'These methodological difficulties sufficiently justify the Judge's conclusion that [the expert's] evidence was neither helpful nor reliable.'

It should be clear that professional witnesses who purport to give 'expert' opinions based solely on their own experience or subjective view do so at their peril. Not only are they in danger of being contradicted by other professionals (either based on their own experience, or on the relevant professional standards), but they may find – as in the cases above – that the court simply refuses to accept their opinion.

In conducting professional research, the expert should consult at least some of the following sources:

Legislative standards

As the world has grown more complex, a need has grown for more complex standards to govern various aspects of our lives. Legislation is now in place in many countries to deal with a variety of day-to-day matters, including: food standards; standards in medicine; standards in mobile telephones; workplace standards; standards for various types of machinery; standards for retention and use of information; and standards for childcare.

While these are matters of law that would normally fall within the expertise of the legal team, it is likely that the experts working in the relevant field would be more familiar with the legislative standards than the legal team instructing them.

If there is legislation that is relevant to the issue in question, the expert should outline it, and reach conclusions by reference to it.

Professional standards

Professional bodies commonly set down codes of conduct or practice guidance for their members. In many cases, these are written for the purpose of dealing with complaints to that body, or its 'fitness to practice' disciplinary measures. However, the same standards can be referred to in other cases. For example, if it could be shown that a client had suffered loss where conduct by a professional had fallen below the standards of their professional body, the court could take this into account when dealing with a negligence action against them.

National and international standards

Standards organisations now exist in many countries, and at a supranational and international level, to ensure that products and services meet certain minimum standards, including safety standards. Professionals working in the relevant fields should reasonably be expected to be familiar with them, and to refer to them in their reports, when reaching conclusions on the relevant issues.

Industry standards

Most industries now have standards for their workers to ensure health and safety. Complex machinery comes with instructions as to its use. If damage or injury has been caused, the professional should refer to these standards also.

Textbooks

Most professions and trades have textbooks that are used both in training and by their members in their professional work. Standard up-to-date textbooks can reasonably be relied upon to reflect the current view of the profession or trade on a particular issue, and should be used by professionals who are asked to provide an objective view of the conduct at issue.

Published articles

A professional is entitled to rely on published articles in seeking to provide an objective standard for the court.

Caution should be used in this regard, however. When a professional publishes an article in a journal, it is often for the purpose of influencing the thinking of the profession, and may be a new theory. If an expert witness seeks to rely on such an article, they should make it clear to the court how the theories in the article fit with the mainstream view of that issue.

Courts tend to be conservative in their determination of contentious issues. Where new theories have been relied upon, they have sometimes led to miscarriages of justice.

In the case of R *v Dallagher*,[4] ear prints had been found on a window at the scene of a murder. The prosecution called an expert who professed to be a specialist in ear prints, and believed that ear prints were unique to each person. He gave evidence that the ear prints matched the ears of the accused. Another professed expert gave similar evidence, although not with the same level of certainty. The accused was convicted. Subsequently, other forensic experts came forward to dispute the reliability of ear prints to identify murder suspects. The conviction was quashed, and a retrial was ordered. At the retrial, DNA from the ear print established that it was not that of the accused, and the charges were dropped.[5]

If expert witnesses are satisfied that a new theory, or a particular published paper, is relevant to the issue to be determined, they should ensure that they have taken all reasonable steps to explain why the orthodox approach might not be applicable.

Comparators

If professional witnesses have been asked to give an opinion on an issue, and there is no published legislative or professional standard on it, they should seek to find some objective basis on which the court might give a determination.

By examining similar systems at work elsewhere, it should be possible to reach some determination as to whether the alleged wrongdoer has fallen below a reasonable standard. However, it would be safest to refer to at least two or three comparators before suggesting that an applicable standard can be inferred by the court.

Ensuring that the professional standards or theories are relevant to the facts

A court is not obliged to accept the theories of a professional witness. An example of this was the trial of Peter Sutcliffe, more commonly known as 'The Yorkshire Ripper', who was charged with the murder of thirteen women, and the attempted murder of seven others.

Following his arrest and questioning, Sutcliffe claimed that he had heard the voice of God instructing him to kill prostitutes. He was examined by four psychiatrists, two for the prosecution and two for the defence. All four of them concluded, independently, that Sutcliffe was suffering from schizophrenia, and that there had been no sexual motive behind the killings. Based on these opinions, the prosecution agreed to accept a plea of guilty to manslaughter, based on 'diminished responsibility'.

The trial judge, unusually, refused to accept this plea, and insisted that the matter be determined by a jury. On cross-examination by counsel for the prosecution, one of the psychiatrists acknowledged that several of Sutcliffe's victims had not been prostitutes and that he had had no reason to have thought that they might be. This undermined the suggested belief in a divine motive. Moreover, certain of the injuries inflicted by Sutcliffe strongly suggested that there was a sexual motive to the killings. Another psychiatrist admitted that he had not considered the prosecution evidence when reaching the conclusion that Sutcliffe suffered from schizophrenia.[6] At the conclusion of the trial, the jury rejected the psychiatrists' conclusions and convicted Sutcliffe of murder. He was sentenced by the judge to life imprisonment, with a recommendation that he serve no less than 30 years.

Conclusion

A professional witness has an obligation to guide the court as to the accepted expertise of the relevant profession or trade. This should be done by reference to accepted standards as set out in published standards, textbooks or other professional literature.

If the professional seeks to rely on novel theories it will be necessary to explain clearly why the more established view is not applicable. And it is essential that any theory fits the facts of the case before the court.

Once the expert has investigated the facts and researched the relevant standards and theories, it is necessary to reach a reliable opinion for the benefit of the court. This is the subject of the next chapter.

Notes

1   *Makita (Australia) Pty Ltd v Sprowles* [2001] NSWCA 305 (NSW Court of Appeal, 14 September 2001).
2   [2020] IECA 138.
3   *Prattley Enterprises Ltd v Vero Insurance New Zealand Ltd* [2016] NZCA 67 (NZ Court of Appeal, Miller J, 14 March 2016).
4   [2002] EWCA Crim 1903.
5   'Earprint landed innocent man in jail for murder' *The Guardian* (23 January 2004).
6   *A Life of Crime* by Harry Ognall, former QC and High Court judge, pp 48–71.

Chapter 7

Reaching a Conclusion

So many problems have arisen concerning expert opinions that a little thought should be given to what type of opinion is being sought, as well as the levels of certainty that may be reached on the subject.

The word 'opinion' derives from the Latin *opinari*, meaning 'think' or 'believe'. In ordinary speech, an opinion is generally considered a subjective matter.

When it comes to court hearings, however, the purpose of an expert 'opinion', is not to inform the court of the subjective belief of the professional, but for the professional to assist the court in reaching a correct inference from the facts before it. The expert's conclusions should not determine the matter, but should inform the court in reaching its own decision.

Types of opinion

Some types of professional opinion are more likely to lend themselves to certainty than others. The following types of opinion are often sought by the court from experts:

Measurable standards

In some cases, professionals are required to use specialist equipment to verify whether certain standards are met. For example, the volume at a place of work can be measured in decibels to test whether it will present a risk to hearing. A building can be measured for levels of damp. A floor can be measured for slipperiness. Providing that the equipment is correctly used, the professional can state with reasonable certainty what the measurement was, and whether it met the relevant standard at the time of measurement.

Diagnoses

Professionals are often required to explain how a particular problem arose, and whether it is consistent with allegations made. Pathologists and other medical professionals are asked to examine injuries to see whether they resulted from alleged wrongdoing or from other causes. Construction professionals are asked to explain how building defects arose. These opinions can be complicated by other factors and pre-existing conditions.

Particular issues have arisen in many countries with psychiatric diagnoses. The definition of some psychiatric conditions is controversial in itself, and some patients have been known to fake or exaggerate the symptoms. As discussed in the previous chapter, in the trial of Peter Sutcliffe (the 'Yorkshire Ripper') four psychiatrists concluded that he suffered from schizophrenia, but the diagnoses was not accepted by the jury. Issues relating to post-traumatic stress disorder (PTSD) often arise in personal injuries cases, and issues relating to dementia often arise in cases concerning the validity of wills and other legal transactions.

Prognoses

The Danish physicist Niels Bohr is reputed to have said: 'Prediction is very difficult, especially about the future.'[1]

Much of the work of a court is likely to involve making informed predictions about the damage suffered in the case, how to remedy it, and what compensation will be required by the injured party. In serious personal injuries cases this may require a range of different professionals, including medical specialists, nursing care specialists, occupational therapists and actuaries. Given the uncertainties of the future of the injured party, and the market in which the person will be operating in the years after the case, the best that can reasonably be expected in relation to many of these issues is an informed guess. The court requires the professionals to act conscientiously, and not to overplay or understate the issues involve.

Estimates of measurable facts

In some cases professionals are required to assist the court in reaching a conclusion as to a fact that would otherwise be measurable. For example, in a case concerning a road traffic accident, an issue may arise as to whether a car was travelling at a high speed. Without any actual reading of the speedometer, the court will have to rely upon the evidence from professionals who examined the damage caused to the vehicles involved or the tyre marks on the road.

Estimates of speculative facts

Where a professional is asked to provide a valuation of land, artworks or livestock, the valuation can rarely amount to more than an educated guess. The court will need to be informed of what the property would have sold for at a particular time in a particular market. Where two valuers reach radically different opinions as to value, it becomes difficult for the court to reach a determination without concrete evidence as to what similar properties actually sold for in similar conditions.

Opinions as to conduct

Where negligence is alleged against a professional, or where a workplace system is alleged to be unsafe, the court will generally be looking at a range of issues to determine whether the defendant has fallen below a particular standard. Having said this, the court will generally be looking at the standard in question from the perspective of the injury or damage that has been suffered, and concluding whether it was foreseeable from the way that the defendant acted.

Forensic 'matches'

Courts rely increasingly on the assistance of forensic science, particularly in criminal cases. For many years, they have relied upon fingerprint experts to give an opinion as to whether a person had been at the scene of a crime or touched a particular item. Handwriting experts have been relied upon to say whether a document was the work of a particular person or whether a signature had been forged. In more recent times, forensic scientists have been used to examine DNA evidence for evidence of identity, or ballistics evidence to see if a person had handled firearms or explosives. While scientific tests have added significantly to the work of criminal investigations, there remains a distinct risk that they will be used to draw the wrong conclusions, as we shall see below.

Artistic or literary judgement

On occasion, controversial works of art have been put 'on trial', generally concerning whether they were obscene or blasphemous. When the album 'Never Mind the Bollocks: Here's the Sex Pistols' was released in 1977, the owner of a record shop in Nottingham was prosecuted for displaying an advertising poster that included the offending word. A linguistics professor from Nottingham University was called to give evidence that 'bollocks' was an Anglo Saxon word, meaning 'small ball', that it appeared in medieval bibles and veterinary books. The accused was acquitted by the magistrate.[2]

Literary experts have been called in trials concerning other controversial works, including DH Lawrences' *Lady Chatterley's Lover* and Hubert Selby Jr's *Last Exit to Brooklyn*. It is reasonable to say that the question of whether a work is 'obscene' is largely a subjective matter. In an arguable case it is questionable whether a judge or jury would require an expert to reach a conclusion on the matter. As the American Supreme Court Justice, Potter Stewart famously said of the term 'hard core pornography' in a trial concerning a film called *The Lovers*:

> I shall not today attempt further to define the kinds of material I understand to be embraced within that shorthand description, and perhaps I could never succeed in intelligibly doing so. But I know it when I see it, and the motion picture involved in this case is not that.[3]

Levels of certainty or probability

The English statistician Dennis Lindley developed a rule known as 'Cromwell's Rule', arising from the famous quotation from Oliver Cromwell in a letter to the General Assembly of the Church of Scotland: 'I beseech you, in the bowels of Christ, think it possible that you may be mistaken.'

The suggestion from Lindley was that any expression of certainty should leave some allowance for the possibility that it may be wrong, or as he put it more charmingly:

> So leave a little probability for the moon being made of green cheese; it can be as small as 1 in a million, but have it there since otherwise an army of astronauts returning with samples of the said cheese will leave you unmoved.[4]

Unwarranted expressions of probability have often troubled the courts. A straightforward example is the 2016 Kenyan case of *Kagina v Kagina*, which concerned the estate of a deceased person. Two document examiners (handwriting experts) examined sales documents, and one of them concluded that it was 'highly probable' that the deceased's signature on one of the documents had been forged. The judge considered this opinion in light of the other evidence of the case, and concluded:

> I have considered the evidence tendered by the document examiner and the report prepared by the said witness and I am persuaded that the said evidence is not build on a sub-stratum of facts *which are proved to the satisfaction of the court according to the appropriate standard of proof.* As stated above, such evidence must be read together with the rest of the evidence but not independently. The evidence by the document examiner in the opinion of this Court does not establish that it is 'highly probable' that the documents in question were forged. (Emphasis in original.)

More problematic have been cases where expressions of probability have been expressed in statistical terms, and these have given rise to some serious miscarriages of justice. They can be divided into three types:

1. Casual use by professionals of statistical language;
2. Incorrectly calculated statistics;

3. Incorrectly presented statistics.

We shall consider each in turn.

Casual use by professionals of statistical language

In 1974, the Provisional Irish Republican Army (IRA) detonated two bombs in pubs in the English city of Birmingham. Twenty-one people were killed and 162 injured. Shortly afterwards, six men who were about to get on a ferry to Belfast were arrested at the Lancashire port of Heysham. The hands of each man were tested for nitroglycerine by forensic scientist, Frank Skuse. Skuse used a test known as the 'Griess test', and found that the hands of two of the men tested positive for the substance.

When the 'Birmingham Six', as they became known, were tried on charges of murder, Skuse testified that he was 'quite happy' that the two men had handled explosives. When asked to define what that meant, he said he was '99.9 per cent certain'. All six were convicted. If they had been convicted a few years earlier, they would have been executed. As it was, they were all sentenced to life imprisonment.

In fact, the 'Griess test' used by Skuse was simply a 'gateway test'. A positive test could have arisen from handling playing cards or even cigarette packets. Furthermore, as established on re-trial, he had not even taken a written note of the results of the test, and did not do until 1987—thirteen years later.[5] There were a number of unsuccessful appeals, but the 'Six' were eventually released in 1991.

What is striking is Skuse's use of the term '99.9 per cent certain', in contrast with the preceding term 'quite happy'. Where a jury is told they can only convict if all members are satisfied of guilt 'beyond a reasonable doubt', the term 'quite happy' arguably leaves room for such doubt. The term '99.9 per cent certain' does not.

In ordinary speech, it is common for people to use percentages to express levels of certainty but without necessarily expecting the listener to treat them as scientific. It is a different matter when a professional in a witness box uses such language before a judge or jury. The decision makers are entitled to assume that the professional has a reasoned or scientific basis for using the term, and are likely to rely on it when making their decision.

A professional who chooses to express a level of certainty in percentage terms should therefore ensure that there is a reasoned basis for it.

Incorrectly calculated statistics

Professor Roy Meadow was a well-known paediatrician, who in 1977 developed the theory of 'Munchausen Syndrome by proxy', where a parent or caregiver makes a child or dependent person appear to be suffering from illness, possibly as a means of attracting attention.[6]

Meadow had also written a book in 1997 entitled *ABC of Child Abuse*. In it he wrote that cases of apparent 'Sudden Infant Death Syndrome' (SIDS, or 'cot death') often arose from the smothering of the child by the mother. He wrote:

> There is now substantial experience of mothers who repetitively smother consecutive children, and reports of mothers killing 3 — or even 9 — children. 'One sudden infant death is a tragedy, two is suspicious and three is murder until proved otherwise' is a crude aphorism but a sensible working rule for anyone encountering these tragedies.

This 'crude aphorism' became known as 'Meadow's Law', and Professor Meadow gave evidence in a number of cases concerning alleged SIDS.

In the case of *R v Clark*,[7] which concerned the mother of two children who had died, Professor Meadow gave evidence that the likelihood of two children dying of SIDS in a family like that of the accused was one in 73 million. He went on to say:

> … it's the chance of backing that long-odds outsider at the Grand National, you know; let's say it's an 80 to 1 chance, you back the winner last year, then the next year there's another horse at 80 to 1 and it is still 80 to 1 and you back it again and it wins. Now here we're in a situation that, you know, to get

> to these odds of 73 million you've got to back that 1 in 80 chance four years running, so yes, you might be very, very lucky because each time it's just been a 1 in 80 chance and you know, you've happened to have won it, but the chance of it happening four years running we all know is extraordinarily unlikely. So it's the same with these deaths. You have to say two unlikely events have happened and together it's very, very, very unlikely.

Professor Meadow had derived the figure of one in 73 million by taking the likelihood of one child dying in an affluent non-smoking household like that of the accused, and squaring it. He was not a statistician, and the basis for his assertion was questionable. Moreover, the statistical likelihood of two children dying within the same family did not amount to a conclusion that one person had necessarily killed either of them, especially if there was an underlying reason for one of the deaths.

Nonetheless, the jury accepted the evidence and found Ms Clark guilty. An appeal in 2000, based on the errors in Professor Meadow's evidence, was dismissed. It later transpired that exculpatory pathological evidence had been withheld from the jury, and Ms Clark's conviction was set aside in 2003. At this stage, the court also acknowledged that the statistical reasoning had been faulty.

So, any professional who seeks to rely on statistical evidence to the court needs to be sure that it has been calculated in a reliable manner.

Incorrectly presented statistics

Even if the statistics as presented to the court have been calculated properly, it is still possible for them to be presented in such a way as to lead to an incorrect conclusion.

The classic example of incorrectly presented statistics is the 'prosecutor's fallacy', which was summed up in the 1996 English case of *R v Doheny*:[8]

> It is easy, if one eschews rigorous analysis, to draw the following conclusion:
> 1. Only one person in a million will have a DNA profile which matches that of the crime stain.

2. The Defendant has a DNA profile which matches the crime stain.

3. Ergo there is a million to one probability that the Defendant left the crime stain and is guilty of the crime.

Such reasoning has been commended to juries in a number of cases by prosecuting counsel, by judges and sometimes by expert witnesses. It is fallacious and it has earned the title of 'The Prosecutor's Fallacy'. ...

Taking our example, the Prosecutor's Fallacy can be simply demonstrated. If one person in a million has a DNA profile which matches that obtained from the crime stain, then the suspect will be one of perhaps 26 men in the United Kingdom who share that characteristic. If no fact is known about the Defendant, other than that he was in the United Kingdom at the time of the crime the DNA evidence tells us no more than that there is a statistical probability that he was the criminal of 1 in 26.

In other words, a statistical probability that a person is one of a number of possible suspects by reason of a DNA match may be presented to a jury as if that person was overwhelmingly likely to be guilty.

Where a professional has established a conclusion to a certain level of probability, it is therefore necessary to ensure that this is correctly presented to the court, so that the judge or jury draw correct inferences from it in reaching their own decision.

The guarded opinion

Having said that the professional should avoid expressing any unwarranted level of certainty, a danger also arises if the professional fails to reach a proper conclusion at all. If a question or issue is central to the case, and the professional has been asked to address it, it is unlikely to assist the court if the professional remains 'on the fence'.

If professionals are unable to reach a reliable conclusion on the issue there is probably a reason for this. It may be that some factual information is not available. It may be that further research is required from the same professionals or other professionals. It may be that the state of expert knowledge is not sufficient to provide the necessary answer.

Where professionals, having examined the factual material and conducted the necessary professional research, are still unable to reach a conclusion on the issue, it would be advisable to set out the reasons for this as clearly as possible.

Once you have considered the relevant facts, and consulted the applicable professional standards or literature, you need to reach a conclusion on the questions asked of you. If the question is one that can be answered to a level of certainty, it is still necessary to explain to the court whether there is any likelihood of a different answer. If using the language of statistics or probability to present your conclusions, you should ensure that the statistics are correctly calculated and correctly presented. Otherwise, there is a significant risk of a miscarriage of justice. Always remember that your role is to assist the court in reaching its own decision on the issue.

Conclusion

A conclusion on the issue for determination should only be reached once the professional has considered all the relevant facts, and applied the appropriate expertise. When expressing an opinion on the issue, the professional should be cautious about the level of certainty involved. If the opinion is expressed as absolute when the facts do not warrant it, the court may well discount the view of the expert. If the expert chooses to use language of statistical probability in expressing an opinion, caution should be used to ensure that this is properly calculated and presented.

When all the factual and professional research has been completed, and the expert has reached a conclusion on the issue at hand, it will be necessary to present this in the form of a report. The next chapter discusses the best ways of approaching this task.

Notes

1 Bohr himself is alleged to have attributed the quotation to Danish writer Robert Storm Petersen (1882–1949), see *The Economist*, Letters 15 July 2007.
2 See Geoffrey Robertson , *The Justice Game* (Random House, 2011) by, p 47.
3 *Jacobellis v Ohio* 378 US 184 (1964).
4 Dennis Lindley, *Making Decisions* (2nd edn, John Wiley & Sons, 1991).
5 See Michael Mansfield, *Memoirs of a Radical Lawyer* (Bloomsbury Publishing, 2009), Chapter 17, for more information on this case.
6 Meadow, 'Munchausen Syndrome by Proxy: The Hinterland of Child Abuse', 2 *Lancet* 343–345 (1977).
7 [2003] EWCA Crim 1020.
8 [1996] EWCA Crim 728.

Chapter 8

Preparing and Writing
an Expert Report

An expert's report is key to the development of any case. In many cases, the better prepared the report is, in terms of investigation and professional research, the less likely it is that the expert will be required to give evidence and to be cross-examined on the report's content.

The purpose of the report is to provide an answer to the questions initially put to the expert. Perhaps more importantly, bearing in mind that the primary duty of the expert is to the court, the report should be the evidence that the expert would give on the issue if called to the witness box.

Readership

The expert should consider the likely readership when writing the report. Judge John Newey QC, a former official referee (construction law judge) has been quoted as having once said: 'If your expert report is not capable of being understood by an intelligent fourteen year old, try again.'[1]

The readers are, of course, unlikely to be fourteen years old, but the writer should bear in mind that they may have a range of educational backgrounds. The report is likely to be read by some or all of the following persons:

The instructing legal team

Members of the instructing legal team will need to read the report and understand its conclusions so they can decide how to pursue the case. It may be that the conclusions of the report lead them to advise the client to discontinue the case altogether, or some aspects of it. They may decide to advise their client to settle for less than the full sum claimed in the case. It will need to be clear to them what conclusions have been reached by the expert, based on what facts, and what research.

While the lawyers are unlikely to be as specialised as the expert, they are likely to be familiar with reports of this sort, and in a position to ask detailed questions.

The client

Any person, or corporate body, could be a party to court proceedings. Some take little interest in the minutiae of the case, leaving it all to the lawyers, while others like to micro-manage every aspect.

It is quite common for lawyers and experts to use language that is unfamiliar to their clients, especially in cases where the clients may have limited formal education. However, the conscientious expert should ensure that the key conclusions in a report are written in a manner that is understandable to the client. Ultimately it will be for the client to make certain important decisions based on the report, such as whether to pursue some aspect of the case.

The legal teams of the other party or parties

Once expert reports have been exchanged between the parties, the legal teams of the other parties will need to read the report to understand its conclusions. Initially, this will be for the purpose of deciding how to pursue the case themselves. In some cases, they may not have their own expert report. Where they do have an expert report, they will need to understand where the experts disagree.

The exchange of reports may lead to a resolution of the case, or some aspect of it. But if the case were to proceed, the legal team for the other party would use the report to prepare to cross-examine the writer. This means that they would study the reports carefully, looking for omissions or inconsistencies that could damage the testimony of the experts or the case their client was trying to make.

The other experts

After the exchange of reports, they are likely to be shared with other expert witnesses. Where the other experts have carried out similar research and prepared reports with different conclusions, they could be 'on the defensive' when reading the report. If they came to different conclusions, they would have to explain to their own client and legal team how this came about, and whether their view had changed on reading the report.

The other experts may also discuss the report in some detail with their instructing legal team while preparations are made for cross-examination.

The judge, arbitrator or other decision maker

When the decision maker is reading the report it will be for the purpose of deciding the case or the relevant issue. Where there are two or more reports, the judge or arbitrator would need to decide between the conclusions in each, probably with the assistance of oral evidence and cross-examination.

Unlike the legal team members, who may have spent months or years working on the case, the judge or arbitrator is likely to be reading the report for the first time at the time of the hearing, along with several other documents concerning the case (pleadings, affidavits and other expert reports). A report that succinctly sets out the issues and explains its conclusions in a readable form is likely to be very welcome.

The jury

Where a report is written for a trial to be decided by jury, the writer should be aware that the jurors will probably come from a range of educational backgrounds. This does not mean that the report should condescend to them, but the writer should be particularly careful to avoid over-technical language if it can be avoided, and to write in a clear manner.

The press (and, via the press, the public)

In most democratic countries, it is a legal requirement that justice be administered in public.

While the open doors of the court allow members of the public to attend, the primary public 'check' on court decisions is the fact that journalists can attend hearings and report on them in the media.

This carries risks of its own. The media tends to sensationalise certain trials, particularly murder trials and those involving high-profile individuals. Occasionally, some aspect of an otherwise ordinary trial will be reported on and will grab the public interest.

Most expert reports are not sensational, and are unlikely to excite the public imagination. But any report that is opened at public hearing may – at least theoretically – be reported in the press. The writer should be aware of this when writing it. For example, it is now common on social media to find discussion of the language used in court, as reported in the press. If language is used that is perceived to be demeaning to a particular group, or, for example, to engage in 'victim blaming', it is common for the person who spoke the words to be publicly admonished for using them.

Other courts or tribunals

Very occasionally, some aspect of a case can 'snowball' into other proceedings. One likely example would be if a professional was accused of misconduct in a case, and the matter was referred to a disciplinary tribunal or led to professional negligence proceedings. Not only might the expert's own report be examined, but so might those of other experts.

In a very different context, Roland Barthes, the French author and literary critic once wrote: 'The birth of the reader must be ransomed by the death of the author.'[2] He meant that once a work is published, the author loses control of it. The reader may infer meaning from the work that is different from that intended by the author.

Where a professional writes a report that is circulated among a number of legal teams, parties and decision makers in a particular case, it could become relevant in a tangential case. Where this occurs, the report could assume a significance other than that originally intended.[3]

Bearing in mind the potential readership, including clients, lawyers, other experts and members of the public, the report would benefit from a clear narrative structure.

Structure of report

However the report is structured, it will be of most use to the readers if, at the outset, it sets out the questions or issues the expert has been asked to address, and, at the end, it concludes with the expert's reasoned answers to them.

Ideally, the body of the report should all be readable by a layperson. If the expert has amassed a quantity of supportive documentation, or prepared extensive calculations, they are best included as appendices. The reader can refer to them as required.

Introduction

At the heading of the report should be basic reference information, including:

- The name of the writer;
- The name of the client;
- The name of the instructing legal firm;
- The name of the case (if proceedings have been issued).

This should be followed by an introductory paragraph that tells the reader what the case is about, and the question that the expert has been asked to address.

To take a few suggested examples:

> This case is a claim for personal injuries where the injured party slipped and fell on a restaurant stairway, on her return from the bathroom. I have been asked to address whether the stairway was unsafe, with particular reference to: the slipperiness of the surface of the stairs; the lack of a handrail on one side of the stairway; the width of the individual stairs; and the lighting of the stairwell.

> This claim is a challenge to the validity of a will, where the testator was 93 years old and had a history of dementia. I have been asked to assess whether he met the criteria for testamentary capacity.

> This claim is for loss of earnings arising from personal injury, where the plaintiff was out of work for several months, and claims to have missed a promotion. I have been asked to calculate the likely loss of earnings she suffered as a result.

It is safest in the introduction to avoid reference to legislation or specialised language. As can be seen from the examples above, it is normally possible to frame the question or issues solidly in laypersons' terms.

Qualifications

The reader will need to know what qualifies the professional to address the particular subject. In this section, the professionals will need to set out their qualifications, together with any specialist training or experience that is relevant to the case.

In some cases, the professionals will have an extensive *curriculum vitae*, including published material and lectures. Where this is likely to cover more than about half a page, it is better to include it as an appendix, summarising the most pertinent elements in the body of the report.

Professionals should avoid exaggerating their qualifications, not least because of the risks involved in doing so. The client or legal team may expect a more learned opinion on matters that are strictly outside the relevant expertise described by the expert. Experts who exaggerate their expertise are likely to be challenged in the witness box, leading to the rest of the testimony being undermined.

Statement of understanding of duty to the court

In many countries, it is now a legal requirement that the writer of the report sets out his understanding of the duties of an expert.

The professional should check with the legal team what the specific requirements are of such a statement, and ensure that it is read and properly understood. On cross-examination, if an expert were to show a lack of understanding of the duty to the court, it could undermine the rest of the evidence.

Experts may also be required in this section to disclose any possible conflicts of interest, or connections with any of the parties to the case. Again, the legal team should be able to outline what disclosure is required.

Facts

The report should clearly set out the facts of the case. Essentially, the writer should concentrate on the facts that are relevant to the question the report is addressing. These may be divided into the following categories.

(a) Background, or uncontested, facts In every case, there are some uncontested facts, such as the date of a road traffic accident, or the names of the parties involved. To set these out helps to set the context for the reader.

(b) Facts received from instructions (hearsay) Where the expert is relying on factual information received from the client or legal team, this will generally be hearsay. The facts in question will need to be given in evidence by witnesses who can directly attest to them. As there is a reasonable likelihood that evidence will be given in court that diverges from the instructions given to the expert, the expert should ensure that any such facts or allegations are set out unambiguously. Where there is an error in the report, the legal team

should be in a position to bring it to the expert's attention so that it may be corrected prior to the hearing of the case.

(c) Facts based on investigations (non-hearsay) The writers can attest to any investigations they have conducted themselves, and the results obtained from them. The report should set these out in a manner that assists the reader to understand them, including context.

The writer should bear in mind that complex information can normally be more readily understood in visual form. Photographs, sketches and graphs will assist the reader.

(d) Contradictions or ambiguities In some cases, the expert may have received contradictory information from two or more witnesses. In other cases, the expert's investigations may suggest that the information received from a client or witness were inaccurate or simply wrong.

An expert witness should not attempt to protect a client or witness who may be seeking to mislead the court. Nor, however, is it the job of the expert to take a moral stance with regard to possible dishonesty. There may be an innocent explanation for any inconsistency.

The safest approach is simply to set out the information in such a manner that any inconsistency is clear to the reader. It will then be for the client and legal team to decide how to deal with it.

(e) Inconvenient facts It is very easy for a professional involved in a case to give little weight to a particular fact or allegation, thinking that the judge or jury will be similarly dismissive. This can be a mistake.

Not only is there a danger that the other side will made a big deal out of something that might seem like a minor issue, but they may also use it to discredit the expert. An expert who fails to mention a particular fact, or treats it as if it is of no consequence, may be accused of a shoddy investigation, or being too wedded to the client's position.

Therefore, before coming to a final conclusion on the facts, it would be advisable to review them in case there is some stubborn fact that might appear to undermine it. Where the inconvenient fact does not affect the conclusion, the report should explain why. Where it does, the conclusion should be amended accordingly.

Relevant professional standards

Where an expert is required to reach a conclusion on the issue, this should be a conclusion that is grounded in the expertise of the profession. It should not be a personal opinion, as this may simply be countered by a different personal opinion expressed by another expert.

Unlike lawyers, who regularly try to persuade courts to accept an interpretation of the law that favours their client, experts are expected to be even-handed, and to give an objective view of their specialist knowledge.

On any question that has been raised, the expert may be expected to have researched the specialist knowledge and applied it to the relevant facts, and to explain it to the decision maker in language that can be understood.

Because law is, in essence, a large collection of rules, lawyers and judges like to have rules and standards from which they can work. Professional witnesses should be able to explain how an experienced and objective member of their profession would approach the question before the court. In order to reach an objective standard or test for the relevant question, it would be advisable to refer to:

- legislative standards (e.g. building regulations);
- professional standards (e.g. codes of conduct);
- industry standards (manuals or safety statements);
- textbooks; and/or
- learned articles.

Where no established test can be found, it might be advisable to look at the practice in other jurisdictions. If this does not assist, the expert should try to find comparators that will assist the decision maker to evaluate the issue.

In some cases, the professional test will also amount to a legal test. Where a building is erected in breach of statutory regulations, no specialist knowledge is required to explain the test, although it is likely to be required in order to show whether the test was breached.

In other cases, the legal test in itself will invite a professional test. For example, to succeed in a professional negligence case, the law will normally require that the conduct of the professional will have fallen below the appropriate standard of the relevant profession. To establish what the standard was will require the expert witness to explain how the profession usually approaches that particular issue, and what type of conduct would be considered unacceptable.

To take a specific example, in the 1999 case of *Penney v East Kent Health Authority*[4] a number of women had been screened for cervical cancer, but it later transpired that the screeners had mistakenly passed their slides as 'negative', when they should have been passed on to a technical checker. The test for professional negligence as established in English law was set out as follows:

> The true test for establishing negligence in diagnosis or treatment on the part of the doctor is whether he has been proved to be guilty of such failure as no doctor of ordinary skill would be guilty of, if acting with ordinary care.[5]

But the court needed to decide what particular test applied to the screeners who had passed the slides as 'negative'. This required experts in the field to establish at what level the passing of a slide as 'negative' would fall below the relevant professional standard. The test that was adopted (which has remained controversial) was that a slide should only be passed as 'negative' if the screener had 'absolute confidence' that it did not contain any abnormalities. In the event, because the slides in question contained obvious abnormalities, the plaintiffs succeeded in their action.

In setting out a professional test, therefore, it is usually necessary for the expert to understand the legal test that the court will be adopting.

If there is a variety of approaches to the question, these should be set out clearly in the report and addressed, so that the decision maker can decide which one is more appropriate to resolving the question.

A reasoned conclusion on the central questions

In the conclusion of the report, the writer should directly address the questions set out in the introduction, and give a clear, reasoned and honest answer to them.

The conclusion should include an acknowledgment of any other answers that might reasonably be given to the questions, and a response to them.

If appropriate, the conclusion should set out any further work that might be done by that professional, or by another professional, to address any aspect of the issue that would benefit from a more conclusive answer.

Length of report: contents pages and appendices

The central body of the report should ideally be short enough, and clearly enough written, that the reader can read it at a single sitting. It is not possible to be prescriptive about length, as some issues are much more complex than others. In a relatively straightforward case, if the main body of the report is likely to be more than ten pages, it may be advisable to revise its length for the benefit of the reader. However, there may be cases where a much longer report is appropriate.

If a report is more than a few pages, a contents page should be included, together with sub-headings.

Appendices can be useful in this regard, as the full material facts can be put in the report without setting them out in monotonous detail in the body. Notes of interviews, tables of measurements, calculations, photographs and other materials obtained during the investigations can all be placed in appendices that are clearly numbered and can be referred to in the body of the report.

Similarly, it may assist the reader to have long passages from textbooks available, or entire chapters of regulations included in the report, but not recited at full length in its main body. These can be included in appendices, with only the most pertinent sections quoted in the body of the report.

A report that is long and cumbersome will be hard to understand for the client, the legal team, the other experts and the judge. It is also likely to take longer to explain to the court, and open the writer to a longer cross-examination.

Blaise Pascal, the 17th century French mathematician and philosopher, once wrote: 'I have made this letter longer than usual, only because I have not had the time to make it shorter.'[6]

Time spent on editing the report for clarity and concision will be time very well spent.

Language and style

Use of clear language is symptomatic of clarity of thought. Where writers set out a problem clearly, outline how they intend to answer it, and then answer it in language the reader can understand, it shows that the writer has clear insight into the problem.

Conversely, if a report is couched in oblique language that the reader finds difficult to follow, it often suggests either that the writer fails to understand the problem or the solution, or that the question is being dodged. The use of long complex sentences is a well-established way of confusing a reader and avoiding accountability, and is particularly favoured by politicians. In the autobiography of Jack Straw, the UK's former foreign secretary, he outlines his approach to being interviewed after George W Bush's 'axis of evil' speech in 2002:

> "I wanted neither to praise the speech nor to damn it. It was time for some unbearably boring quotes. Thank God for the compound sentence; the subordinate clause."[7]

It is easy to tell a writer to write clearly, but not always as easy to explain how it should be done. Some helpful books on the subject are listed at the end of this chapter.

The following are a few pointers to bear in mind when editing a report for clarity:

Technical language

Every profession, of necessity, has technical language that is difficult for a layperson to understand. In a report for court proceedings, this language needs to be translated so that a layperson can understand it.

Where the layperson's term can be used throughout the report, with no loss of meaning, this is always preferable. If it is necessary to use the technical term, however, it must be explained on the first time of use, so that the reader can learn it and – where necessary – refer back to the explanation when it is forgotten. For example: 'The patient was suffering from hypertension (high blood pressure). She gave a history of epistaxis (nosebleeds) on an almost daily basis.'

If many technical terms need to be used in the body of the report, the best approach is to include a glossary.

Some professionals may be so familiar with technical language that they can forget that it is not a part of normal speech. It is not difficult to find out whether such terms are familiar. Friends and family members outside the relevant specialisation can be relied upon to tell the writer whether they understand a particular term.

Industry jargon, or slang

Slang has no place in a formal court report. Sometimes it can make a report seem flippant. Sometimes slang terms can be ambiguous, in that they may have a different meaning in a different industry or profession. But the main reason not to use slang or jargon is that it is likely to make the writer seem less serious. Informality in speech can make the speaker seem friendlier, but informality in prose – unless written to a personal friend – can come across as sloppy.

Abbreviations and acronyms

In June 2017, the World Taekwondo Federation, which had been founded in 1973, changed its name. The acronym 'WTF', which it had been accustomed to using as shorthand, had taken on a new meaning in social media by then, and the organisation deemed it prudent to change the name simply to World Taekwondo, or WT.[8]

It is all too common in professional reports to find acronyms used without explanation, and there is always a danger of ambiguity. However familiar they are to the writer, even such familiar acronyms as USA or UK should probably be spelled out on the first time of use.

With widely-used abbreviations, there may be some (mm, cm, km, kg) that are so familiar that an explanation is unnecessary. Others, such as kJ (kilojoules) or dB (decibels) should be spelled out on the first time of use.

Sentences

Sentences should normally be kept short. Long sentences with several sub-clauses can often be divided into two or more sentences. This exercise can make it easier for the reader to understand the content.

Having said this, prose made up entirely of very short sentences can be monotonous to read. A mix of longer and shorter sentences is preferable. A useful test is to read the passage out loud to hear how the sentences sound when read together.

Paragraphs

Paragraphs should be numbered. During a court hearing, it is common for all the participants to be referred to a particular passage of a particular document. If the paragraphs, as well as the pages, are numbered, it is far easier for everybody to find the relevant passage.

Paragraphs should also be kept relatively short. Those that run to more than about five sentences, or take up more than about a quarter of an A4 printed page, can conceal their main point.

Descriptions of parties

A common fault in legal documents is that parties can be described in such a way that the reader can be confused as to their identity. In the initial hearing, they may be described as 'plaintiff', or 'claimant', and 'defendant'; or 'applicant' and 'respondent'. On appeal, they may be described as 'appellant' and 'respondent'. Confusion can arise if it is not clear to the reader who the 'appellant' actually is.

As a rule of thumb the clearest way of describing the parties is as they relate to each other in the context of the case: eg employer and employee; landlord and tenant; driver and injured party; police officer and suspect.

Use of verbs

When trying to make a complex sentence or clause more understandable, a useful technique is to move the main operative verb closer to the subject noun.

Take the following sentence:

> The High Court, in considering a personal injuries case that turned on the issue of whether a supermarket floor was slippery where the injured party

> had been wearing high heels, dismissed it on the grounds that the engineer who was acting for her had failed to refer to the appropriate industry standards.

A reader who is unfamiliar with the subject matter might have to read the sentence two or three times to realise that the operative verb is 'dismissed'. By moving the verb closer to the main subject noun (the High Court), the sentence becomes more understandable:

> The High Court **dismissed** a personal injuries case that turned on the issue of whether a supermarket floor was slippery, where the injured party had been wearing high heels, on the grounds that the injured party's engineer had failed to refer to the appropriate industry standards.

The last clause could also be re-written as a new sentence, but by moving the verb 'failed' closing to the subject noun ('engineer'), the clause becomes easier to read.

Use of adjectives and adverbs

Where adjectives and adverbs are used to modify other terms it is best to keep them close to the terms they are modifying. Take the following example:

> Because it was bright red, when Fred drove past the store, his car was noticed by everyone.

A reader may need to read the sentence twice to be sure that it was the *car*, rather than the store, that was red. The sentence can be rewritten as follows, and any ambiguity will be removed:

> Because Fred's car was bright red, it was noticed by everyone when he drove past the store.

Use of negatives

Professionals often use negatives where they could be avoided, and where the proposition would be phrased better in positive terms. To take the following examples:

- 'not many people' may be rephrased as: 'few people';
- 'is not the same' may be rephrased as: 'is different';
- 'does not have' may be rephrased as: 'lacks';
- 'did not consider' may be rephrased as: 'ignored'

Use of emphatic language

Occasionally, a simple rephrasing of a sentence can make the underlying proposition sound fresher and more emphatic. For example:

'Do not ask what your country can do for you …' may be rephrased as: 'Ask not what your country can do for you …;

'If the architect had carried out the inspection properly, he would have found …' may be rephrased as: 'Had the architect carried out the inspection properly, he would have found …';

'Other subjects could be looked into.' may be rephrased as: 'Other subjects could be explored.'

Inclusive language

Traditionally, it was considered acceptable in many forums to use masculine language ('he' and 'him') to refer to people of either sex. Particularly in legal documents, where legislation or contracts referred to a hypothetical person, that person was generally treated as male. It was understood that 'he' also meant 'she', and that 'him' also meant 'her'. This is increasingly considered unacceptable.

Moreover, other language that was routinely used in everyday speech, and in the media, is now recognised to cause offence or discomfort to marginalised groups. For example, it has been common to use terms relating to disability as metaphors.

While some people may dismiss these concerns as 'political correctness', it is important to recognise that language evolves over time. It would be unfortunate if an otherwise well-researched and well-written report were subject to extensive criticism in court because of phraseology that was no longer considered acceptable.

Many organisations now publish guidelines on inclusive language, and the word-processing programme Microsoft Word now includes an 'inclusiveness' setting in its 'proofing' function.

General

The writer should aim to present a report that is authoritative, and can be understood by laypersons and professionals alike. The report should be clear as to its purpose, the methods adopted by the writer, and the conclusions reached.

Once the report is submitted, however, a request may come from the legal team for a follow-up or supplemental report.

Supplemental reports

> It is highly undesirable that a decision based on an inadequate report prepared by an expert should stand when the expert, long before trial, asserts by a further report that he has been misunderstood or that on the receipt of further material he has been able to clarify, expand or modify his opinion. In such a case, in my view, justice would demand the admission of that evidence.[9] (*Salzke v Khoury*, Court of Appeal of New South Wales)

Having worked hard to prepare a report at the request of a legal team, some dismay can be caused to the expert some days or weeks later when a letter arrives asking for another report, or for the original report to be clarified. But this is often necessary.

A further report may be required for any of the following reasons:

a) The legal team may not have understood the conclusions in the report, and may require clarification.
b) The expert may have omitted, or given insufficient weight to a key fact.
c) New facts may have emerged.
d) The expert may have failed to address a central question in the report.
e) An issue may have been raised in correspondence or pleadings

that needs to be addressed by the expert.

f) The legal team may have received a report from the other side that it now wants the expert to address.

g) The expert may have made a mistake.

It is common for professionals to be a little defensive when receiving requests of this sort, either because they think their existing report is quite adequate, or because they suspect that the legal team is trying to prompt them to give a particular answer.

Nevertheless, it is the job of the legal team to ensure that the expert has addressed the question properly, and sometimes it is necessary to seek a further report. Generally, an expert who has provided a fee estimate will be entitled to proper payment for any work on a supplemental report. An expert who has made an error in the original report might be wiser not to pursue payment for any work necessary to correct it.

If, in the light of the further instructions received, the expert has a change of mind on a key issue concerning the case, it is best that it be established at an early stage. Otherwise, much time and money could be expended by both sides before the matter comes to light.

Where an expert has made a serious mistake in the initial report, and this has only been realised at a later stage of the proceedings, the implications could be serious. If the client has spent considerable resources pursuing a case that needs to be discontinued or settled at a lower value, it is possible that recourse will be sought from the expert. While different countries have different rules in relation to such exposure, the expert should consider whether the mistake was such as to warrant notifying their insurer, seeking guidance from their professional body, or obtaining independent legal advice.

If there are complex matters to discuss arising from the initial report, it might be preferable for the expert and legal team to have a face-to-face consultation prior to the preparation of a supplemental report. This gives them the opportunity to clear up any misunderstanding, and can avoid the awkwardness that can arise from the request for a supplemental report.

Further Reading

There are several books and articles on writing style that may be useful. For a very helpful – and very short – article with guidelines on writing, see 'The Elements of Plain Language', by Joseph Kimble, *Michigan Bar Review*, October 2002. (This is available for free online, and is one of a series of articles on plain language in legal documents.) Otherwise:

- Joseph Williams, *Style: Toward Clarity and Grace* (University of Chicago Press, 1995).
- Joseph Williams and Gregory Columb, *The Craft of Argument* (Pearson, 2006).
- *The Economist Style Guide: The bestselling guide to English usage* (Economist Books, 12th edn, 2018).
- Benjamin Dreyer, *Dreyer's English: An utterly correct guide to clarity and style* (Century, 2019).
- Mark Forsyth, *Elements of Eloquence* (Icon Books, 2014).

Notes

1   'How to get the best from your Expert–Practical advice for Instructing Solicitors' *The Expert Witness Journal*, 21 August 2019.

2   'The Death of the Author' by Roland Barthes, *Aspen: The Magazine in a Box*, issue 5+6, 1967.

3   In Ireland, an example of this arose in a tribunal of inquiry concerning allegations of police corruption, known as the Disclosures Tribunal. A whistleblower had been subject to an investigation of sexual assault. Because of an error by a psychologist in her report on the alleged assault, the whistleblower was subject of a much more serious allegation, giving rise to false rumours among his colleagues and superiors. The psychologist was called to give evidence, and cross-examined as to whether she had deliberately forwarded the false allegation to other parties. 'Counsellor denies she was part of conspiracy' *The Irish Independent* (6 July 2017).

4   [1999] EWCA Civ 3005 (16 November 1999).

5   *Maynard v West Midland Regional Health Authority* [1984] 1WLR 634.

6   Blaise Pascal, *The Provincial Letters* (1657), Letter XIV.

7   Jack Straw, *Last Man Standing: Memoirs of a Political Survivor* (Macmillan, 2012), p 366.

8   'WTF, FML and a brief history of sporting initialisms and acronyms' *The Guardian* (26 June 2017).

9   *Salzke v Khoury* [2009] NSWCA 195 (NSW Court of Appeal, 10 August 2009).

Chapter 9

Communication and Consultation Between the Experts and the Instructing Legal Team

At some stage between the initial retainer of the expert and the trial of the action a meeting between the expert and the legal team is likely to be necessary. In complex cases, there may be many such meetings.

There will be other communication. The experts may be required to send supplemental reports. Questions may be raised on the content of the report. Some communications may be exchanged by way of email, with friendly covering messages. The expert may know the client or members of the legal team from having worked with them on other cases, and there may be opportunities to discuss the case at other events.

At no stage during the process, however, should the expert forget that the primary duty is to the court rather than the client or legal team. The expert should not try to assist the client to win the case, but should answer any questions honestly and with the benefit of the relevant specialist knowledge.

Not only should experts ensure that any report and oral evidence represents their honest view concerning the case, they should ensure that no communications between them and the legal team either compromise their impartiality or allow any other person to question it.

Consultations

> While some degree of consultation between experts and legal advisers is entirely proper, it is necessary that expert evidence presented to the court should be, and should be seen to be, the independent product of the expert, uninfluenced as to form or content by the exigencies of litigation. To the extent that it is not, the evidence is likely to be not only incorrect but self defeating.[1] (*Whitehouse v Jordan,* United Kingdom House of Lords)

> Trained solicitors and barristers involved in pre-trial consultations will avoid any suggestion to a witness that a particular emphasis is needed in evidence, much less suggest that a witness should embroider or invent facts. The nature of this process, if professionally conducted, is neutral. It does no more than focus potential evidence and it avoids directing its content. Formal enquiry in preparation for trial is necessary and appropriate: it can help expose strengths and weaknesses to the professional lawyers representing a client; this, when conducted in this neutral form, aids a fair assessment prior to court, possible settlement of a case and its proper prosecution at trial. Witnesses are never to be directed as to the content of their evidence. It would fundamentally undermine the trial process were it to be allowed to become fictional whereby each side is presenting invented facts based on direction as to what may assist their case.[2] (*O'R v DPP,* High Court of Ireland)

The general rule is that clients and legal teams may consult with their witnesses (expert or otherwise), providing that they do not attempt to influence the evidence that they give.

It will be noted that in *Whitehouse v Jordan,* quoted above, the House of Lords said that the expert evidence should be uninfluenced as to 'form or content' by the exigencies of litigation. As will be clear from other material in this chapter, the general view is that the legal team can assist an expert in relation to the presentation of the evidence, both in the report and—to a certain extent—in the witness box.

Nonetheless, the expert should in no way be prompted to give a particular answer to a particular question. As far as possible, the legal team should avoid indicating which answer they would like to get. Having said this, the expert would not need to be particularly shrewd to guess in most cases what the more convenient answer would be. Some consultations take place in quite fraught conditions (during pre-trial settlement talks and during mediation), and the reaction to a particular answer is likely to tell experts all that is needed to know as to whether it was helpful to their own side. But the experts' primary duty is to the court, and the evidence should not be given in a manner intended to assist the instructing party.

The expert should also avoid getting involved in 'litigation tactics'. Depending on the type of case, and the forum in which it is to be heard, the legal team may decide that it would be convenient for the expert, say, to delay the preparation of a report. These are matters that should more safely be left to the legal team. If expert witnesses engage in such tactics it would compromise their independence.

The safest course of action would be for minutes to be kept of any consultation between experts and the legal team, so that all parties have a reliable note of what took place. In practice, it is rare for such formality to be adopted. It would therefore be advisable for all parties to keep a note of what was discussed in any consultation or telephone conversation.

In particular, if an expert after such a consultation feels that there might have been a misunderstanding of the advice given, it would be prudent to send clarification by way of a letter.

Correspondence

In any correspondence between the expert and the legal team, it would be advisable to adopt an 'arms length' tone. Bearing in mind that the expert should be impartial and that the legal team is acting in the client's interest, the expert should be scrupulous in avoiding any suggestion that the report or evidence is for the client's benefit.

In practice, it may be easy to fall into bad habits. Experts may often have dealings with the same legal team in a number of cases. While the report may be written in a formal manner, it might be sent to the legal team under cover of an informal email.

Generally, such emails are unlikely to be disclosed to other parties. But, as discussed in the section on disclosure and privilege later in this chapter, there may be occasions when they do come under scrutiny. A covering email might, for instance, say: 'I am sorry that the attached report is not more helpful to your client.' This might be overlooked at a human level, but could be construed to suggest that the expert was sympathetic to the client.

Worse would be an email that says: 'I hope the enclosed report helps your client's case.' If the conduct of the professional in the case was subject to any review, the email would certainly be understood to suggest that the expert was not acting in a strictly impartial manner.

Most such communications between the expert and the legal team will never be read by other parties. But in the rare cases where an expert is accused of improper conduct, the inquiring court or tribunal may have reason to seek emails and notes concerning the case. Prudent experts will therefore ensure that no correspondence contains any 'hostages to fortune' that might damage their professional reputation.

Revisions by lawyers to expert reports

Lawyers should be involved in the writing of reports by experts: not, of course, in relation to the substance of the reports (in particular, in arriving at the opinions to be expressed); but in relation to their form, in order to ensure that the legal tests of admissibility are addressed.[3] (*Harrington-Smith v Western Australia (No 2)*, Federal Court of Australia)

Counsel play a crucial mediating role by explaining the legal issues to the expert witness and then by presenting complex expert evidence to the court. It is difficult to see how counsel could perform this role without engaging in communication with the expert as the report is being prepared. Leaving the expert witness entirely to his or her own devices, or requiring all changes to be documented in a formalized written exchange, would result in increased delay and cost in a regime already struggling to deliver justice in a timely and efficient manner. Such a rule would encourage the hiring of 'shadow experts' to advise counsel. There would be an incentive to jettison rather than edit and improve badly drafted reports, causing added cost and delay. Precluding consultation would also encourage the use of those expert witnesses who make a career of testifying in court and who are often perceived to be hired guns likely to offer partisan opinions, as these expert witnesses may require less guidance and preparation.[4] (*Moore v Getahun*, Court of Appeal of Ontario)

It may come as a surprise to some that courts would countenance the involvement of lawyers in the drafting or revisions to expert reports. But it is clear from the case law of Australia and Canada that such involvement may not only be allowed but even encouraged.

Where a legal team seeks to discuss the content of the report before it is written, or to revise it prior to communication, the expert must be vigilant to ensure that the substance has remained unaltered. The reason for such involvement is to assist the court to reach the correct decision. If the report contains inadmissible material, for example, a legal issue may arise at hearing where the court is asked to exclude it. If the report is excessively long, or badly drafted, it may take more court time than is necessary to discuss it, which may provide more opportunities for the other legal team to cross-examine at length.

Following any such consultation or revision, a report should only be approved by an expert who is satisfied that it is an accurate account of the facts, expertise and conclusions of that expert. No sleight of hand should be used to suggest that the expert's view is different from that actually reached.

Disclosure and privilege

> In my view, the ends of justice do not permit litigation privilege to be used to shield improper conduct. As I have already mentioned, it is common ground on this appeal that it is wrong for counsel to interfere with an expert's duties of independence and objectivity. Where the party seeking production of draft reports or notes of discussions between counsel and an expert can show reasonable grounds to suspect that counsel communicated with an expert witness in a manner likely to interfere with the expert witness's duties of independence and objectivity, the court can order disclosure of such discussions.[5] (*Moore v Getahun*, Court of Appeal of Ontario)

Privilege is the rule of law that allows one party to refuse to disclose documents to the other party or parties in a case.

In most common law countries, privilege comes under two broad categories: 'legal advice privilege' (or 'solicitor–client privilege'); and 'litigation privilege'.

Legal advice privilege covers most correspondence between a client and the solicitor or legal team, whether or not it was relevant to litigation.

Litigation privilege, on the other hand, covers any communication where the 'dominant purpose' of the communication is litigation or anticipated litigation.[6]

In general, in most countries, litigation privilege does cover communications between the expert and the client or legal team. This would include emails, notes of telephone conversations and any drafting assistance given by the legal team to the expert in the drafting of the report.

It would be foolhardy for any expert to rely on privilege to say or write anything that compromised his or her impartiality.

Firstly, the conduct of the expert could come under scrutiny in other proceedings. If a professional negligence case arose, or if there was a complaint about the expert's professional body, privilege would be unlikely to apply to any such communications. The expert's conduct could well be in question if inappropriate comments were recorded.

Secondly, as discussed in the quotation above from the 2015 Canadian case of *Moore v Getahun*, litigation privilege cannot be used as a 'shield' for improper conduct. If, in the relevant proceedings, a reasonable suspicion is raised that the legal team engaged in inappropriate redrafting of the expert report, it would be open to the court to insist on the production of any relevant notes, draft reports or emails.

Finally, some countries have different rules on privilege. In Ireland, for example, there is effectively no privilege for communications with experts in High Court personal injuries actions. Arising from concerns over the conduct of such actions, the law was amended in 1995 to provide that each party should disclose to the other any expert reports that were to be used in the case, to include other reports and correspondence from the expert 'containing the substance of the evidence to be adduced'.[7]

Experts should therefore be cautious not to allow any communication with the legal team to compromise their independence and objectivity. Experts should be impartial, and they should be seen to be impartial.

Training of expert witnesses

There is a dramatic distinction between witness training or coaching, and witness familiarisation. Training or coaching for witnesses in criminal proceedings (whether for prosecution or defence) is not permitted. This is the logical consequence of well-known principle that discussions between witnesses should not take place, and that the statements and proofs of one witness should not be disclosed to any other witness. The witness should give his or her own evidence, so far as practicable uninfluenced by what anyone else has said, whether in formal discussions or informal conversations. … [T]he principle does not prohibit training of expert and similar witnesses in, for example, the technique of giving comprehensive evidence of a specialist kind to a jury, both during evidence-in-chief and in cross-examination, and, another example, developing the ability to resist the inevitable pressure of going further in evidence than matters covered by the witnesses' specific expertise. The critical feature of training of this kind is that it should not be arranged in the context of nor related to any forthcoming trial, and it can therefore have no impact whatever on it.[8] (*R v Momodou*, Court of Appeal of England and Wales)

Witnesses who are unfamiliar with court proceedings can be understandably nervous about taking the stand and facing a litany of questions from the barristers on either side of the case. They might understandably wish to rehearse their performance with the legal team instructing them, and to discuss the answers they might consider giving on cross-examination. This is generally not permitted, although the rules vary according to country. In the US, witness preparation is broadly permitted, although lawyers are not entitled to tell the witness to give a false answer.[9] In Britain and Ireland, the rule is strictly that witnesses may not be coached.[10] The fear is that the legal team will simply prepare the witness to give the answers they want.

In *R v Momodou*, quoted above, witnesses for the prosecution had attended a training course. They were employees of a private security firm working under contract in a prison. The manner in which the 'training' was conducted was admitted by the prosecution to have been inappropriate.

An exercise known as 'familiarisation' is permitted, however, whereby witnesses may be shown the court room in advance of the hearing. The court procedure may be explained to them, and they may be told, for example, that short and direct answers may be preferable to longwinded ones. This exercise should help to reassure a nervous witness, while not addressing the actual evidence to be given.

Because expert witnesses are in a different category from other witnesses, generally giving evidence concerning their specialisation, they may be 'trained', but not in the context of an individual case. Any potential expert witnesses are likely to benefit from such an exercise, so that they understand what is required of a court report, and what they are likely to experience when giving their evidence in chief and when being cross-examined.

An expert witness who is asked to go further and attend a rehearsal or training session in respect of evidence to be given in a particular case should clarify whether such 'training' is acceptable in the relevant jurisdiction.

Conclusion

Providing that the expert witness and the instructing legal team understand the proper nature of the relationship between them, no issue should arise. The expert is not a member of the legal team, and the legal team has no role in directing the substance of the expert's evidence, either directly or by implication, aside from ensuring that the relevant issue is properly addressed.

On this basis, communication between the expert and the legal team should always maintain a professional distance. If it is allowed to slip too much into informality, there is a danger that the distinction between the roles may be compromised.

Different considerations arise when expert witnesses are required to meet the experts for the other parties, as we shall see.

Notes

1   *Whitehouse v Jordan* [1980] UKHL 12 (United Kingdom House of Lords, 17 December 1980).

2   *O'R v DPP* [2011] IEHC 368 (High Court of Ireland, Charleton J, 7 October 2011).

3   *Harrington-Smith v Western Australia (No 2)* (2003) 130 FCR 424.

4   *Moore v Getahun* 2015 ONCA 55 (Ontario Court of Appeal, Sharpe JA, 29 January 2015).

5   *Moore v Getahun* (2015) ONCA 55 (Ontario Court of Appeal, Sharpe JA, 29 January 2015).

6   *Blank v Canada (Minister of Justice)* (2006) SCC 39 (CanLII); [2006] 2 SCR 319; *Esso Australia Resources v Commissioner of Taxation* [1999] HCA 67; 201 CLR 49; 168 ALR 123; 74 ALJR 339 (21 December 1999).

7   See s 45 of the Courts and Court Officers Act 1995; SI 391 of 1998; and *Payne v Shovlin* [2006] IESC 5.

8   *R v Momodou* [2005] EWCA Crim 177 (Court of Appeal of England and Wales, Judge LJ, 2 February 2005).

9   *State v McCormick* 259 S.E. 2d 880 (1979).

10 The Code of Conduct of the Bar of England and Wales states, at rule c9.4: 'you must not rehearse, practise with or coach a witness in respect of their evidence.' The Bar of Ireland's Code of Conduct states: 'Barristers may not coach a witness in respect of evidence to be given.'

Chapter 10

Meetings with Other Experts

Courts generally look favourably upon meetings between expert witnesses representing each party to a case. Such meetings are designed to establish the areas of agreement and disagreement between the experts, so that the court can establish clearly what needs to be decided.

Before an expert engages in such a meeting, the following matters should be established:

a) the reason for the meeting;
b) whether the meeting has been agreed between the parties or directed by the court;
c) the stage of the proceedings at which the meeting has been called;
d) whether the experts should meet 'on site';
e) whether the meeting is to be held 'without prejudice';
f) whether either party or legal team should be present;
g) whether a joint report is to be prepared.

The reason for the meeting

In general, meetings between experts are arranged for the purposes of narrowing the issues between them. In other words, the experts should attempt to establish what relevant facts are agreed and what are not agreed.

But meetings could be directed or agreed for other reasons. For example, in the 2003 Irish case of *McGrory v Electricity Supply Board*[1] the Irish Supreme Court granted a stay on a personal injuries action pending a meeting between the injured party's treating doctors and the expert medical witnesses acting for the defendant. This was for the purpose of obtaining factual information concerning the relevant medical condition, rather than to delimit the areas of disagreement between experts.

Before the expert attends any meeting, it would be advisable to establish from the legal team what the purpose of the meeting is, and whether there is any particular agenda to be discussed or agreed.

Whether the meeting has been agreed between the parties or directed by the court

In most countries, the courts have the power to direct a meeting between expert witnesses. The terms of such a meeting will either be set down in the relevant legislation or rules or court, or the court order will set down the matters to be addressed.

If the meeting has been agreed between the parties, the expert should establish from them whether the meeting should operate according to court rules, or whether other parameters have been agreed.

The stage of the proceedings at which the meeting has been called

If a meeting has been arranged prior to the issue of proceedings, or before pleadings are closed, it is likely to be exploratory in nature. Each side will be trying to establish whether the case is worth either pursuing or defending. This does not necessarily mean that the meeting will be more cordial, but a full and frank discussion between experts at an early stage could resolve some of the issues.

If the meeting occurs after pleadings have closed, or after an exchange of expert reports, each side is likely to have committed considerable resources to the case. They are likely to be committed to particular factual positions, and there could be consequences for any change of mind.

This does not in any way detract from the duty of the expert to the court to give an honest opinion in relation to each such issue. But any expert attending a joint meeting should be aware that a change of mind at a later stage of the proceedings may have more serious implications for the client.

Whether the experts should meet 'on site'

Where the experts are meeting 'on site' or having a joint inspection of any matter relevant to the proceedings, certain issues should be agreed in advance. For example, it might be an opportunity to agree certain factual matters, such as measurements. Rather than each expert conducting measurements individually, and reporting on them separately, it would assist the factual resolution of the case if they were to agree the measurements there and then, to ensure that the decision maker is given reliable information that will not be disputed by either side.

Similarly, the experts might seek to agree the matters to be photographed or sketched, and agree notes concerning descriptive matters.

A procedure for agreeing such factual matters should be agreed in advance; for example, measurements and sketches could be initialed by each expert to show that they have agreed them.

Whether the meeting is to be held 'without prejudice'

When a meeting is held and it is agreed, or directed, that it be 'without prejudice', it is important that the experts understand the implications of this. A 'without prejudice' meeting is comparable to an 'off the record' briefing to a journalist. The purpose is to allow the discussion to be full and frank, but without consequences for anybody who might make a damaging admission.

Where any statements (whether written or oral) are stated to be 'without prejudice', they cannot be given in evidence against the party making them. Expert witnesses in a joint meeting might admit in discussions that they did not believe the client had a good case, and that their report was more positive than it should be. If the meeting was 'without prejudice', that statement could not be used against the expert in cross-examination.

It is generally considered advisable for such meetings to be conducted 'without prejudice' so that the experts can discuss matters in detail without fear that any unguarded comment might be misconstrued as an admission.

Whether either party or legal team should be present

As a general rule, meetings between experts do not involve the clients or legal teams. If the legal teams are present, they are more likely to be vigilant for unguarded statements, or indications that the experts on the other side are wavering in their confidence in their opinion.

There may be circumstances, however, where other persons should be present during part of such a meeting. In a personal injuries case, it is reasonably common for the experts on either side to reach a different understanding of how the accident took place. If the injured party attends on-site to show both experts where and how the accident happened, it can avoid a misunderstanding that could otherwise linger until the hearing of the action.

In other circumstances, a discussion between the experts and both legal teams might be beneficial. For example, if a mediation were agreed, and there was deadlock over an issue relating to expert evidence, it might be suggested by the mediator that a discussion between the legal teams and the experts would assist to establish the parameters of the dispute in question. It is likely that such a meeting would be conducted 'without prejudice'.

Whether a 'joint report' is to be prepared

Where a joint report is to be prepared, it is generally for the benefit of the decision maker—to establish which facts or theories are agreed between the experts, and which are not.

The joint report is likely to form the 'agenda' for the court when it comes to resolving the expert evidence, especially if 'concurrent evidence' ('hot-tubbing') is directed.

If asked to agree a joint report with the expert for the other side, the professional should be co-operative but not naive. If the report is initially drafted by the other side's expert, it should be read in fine detail to ensure that no concessions are inadvertently made. Even slight concessions made in a joint report are likely to be damaging for the party instructing the expert, and it is unlikely that the position will be improved in oral evidence.

If several drafts of a joint report are exchanged between the experts, particular caution should be adopted before signing a final draft, in case small changes have been made to the body of the report.

Before experts agree a joint report, they should compare it with their own initial report, to ensure that the they are clear as to what changes may have been made. It should be borne in mind that the 2011 English case of *Jones v Kaney,*[2] which concerned the liability of expert witnesses, arose from a joint report that changed the position of an expert—thus leading the injured party to settle a case for a lower sum.

Conclusion

Meetings between experts are a valuable opportunity to clarify issues that might otherwise take substantial court time to resolve. Conducted properly, each expert will act 'in good faith' to ensure that any differences of opinion are clear and explainable to the decision maker. But such meetings are likely to lead to changes of mind by experts, with consequences for their clients. If a change of mind occurs, it should be communicated to the legal team, and then to the legal team for the other party. But the expert attending such a meeting should be wary of making concessions without sufficient consideration.

In addition to preparing reports, and joint reports, the expert may be required to assist in the preparation of other documents, as will be outlined in the next chapter.

Notes

[1]   [2003] IESC 45.

[2]   *Jones v Kaney* [2011] UKSC 13.

Chapter 11

Pleadings, Affidavits and 'Scott Schedules'

Between the commencement of an action and the case going to final hearing, a number of documents need to be produced. Chief among these from the experts' point of view, is the initial report, although this may give rise to such things as supplemental reports, answers to questions from other legal teams, and reports written jointly with other experts.

As well as the experts' own reports, other documents will be produced during a case, some of which may require expert involvement. Among the most important of these are pleadings and affidavits. In many cases, these will not require any expert involvement at all. In others, extensive consultation will be required with experts to ensure that the detail in the documents is correct.

In some cases, the parties to the case are required to furnish a joint document called a 'Scott Schedule', which is likely to involve detailed expert involvement.

Pleadings

The pleadings in a case are the statements of fact made by each party to underpin the claim and defence. They are the documents in which the parties set out the allegations they intend to rely upon. Each party, prior to hearing, is entitled to know the case that they are likely to meet.

The plaintiff—or claimant—issues a document usually called a 'statement of claim', which sets out the allegations in a structured form, to establish that the plaintiff is entitled to the relief claimed against the defendant. For example, if a party is seeking damages for breach of contract, it will be normally be necessary to establish:

a) that a legally binding contract was agreed between the plaintiff and defendant;
b) that the contract contained certain relevant terms;
c) that the relevant contractual terms were breached by the defendant;
d) that the breach of the contractual terms caused loss to the plaintiff; and
e) that the plaintiff is entitled to recover compensation from the defendant arising from the losses.

In response to the statement of claim, the other party issues a document, usually called a 'defence', which sets out why they believe that are not liable to pay damages to the plaintiff. The defence may simply amount to a denial of the allegations (which means that the plaintiff would be put to the expense of proving each element of the claim), or may include specific reasons why each point of claim should not succeed.

To take the example above, the defendant might contend as follows:

a) that any agreement between the parties was not intended to be legally binding;
b) that the alleged agreement did not contain the alleged terms, or that the terms did not have the meaning contended for;
c) that the conduct of the defendant did not amount to a breach of the terms, or that it was the result of wrongdoing by a third party that was outside the control of the defendant;
d) that any losses suffered by the plaintiff were not caused by any breach of contract by the defendant, but had another cause; or
e) that the plaintiff was not legally entitled to recover any alleged losses against the defendant (e.g. because the contract excluded such recovery).

The statement of claim needs to show sufficient allegations to 'disclose a cause of action' against the other party. In other words, it needs to be drafted in such a way as to show that it complies with the legal requirements to succeed in the case. If the statement of claim does not disclose a cause of action courts are generally entitled to dismiss the case without going to hearing.

From the defendant's point of view, if the defence is not drafted in such a way as to show that it has a reasonable chance of success courts are entitled to strike out it out and enter judgment against the defendant in question. Pleadings must therefore be drafted carefully by the legal teams to ensure that they include sufficient allegations of fact to support the cause of action or defence.

Non-judicial bodies, such as arbitrations, and quasi-judicial bodies, such as employment tribunals, or tax appeal tribunals, will generally have an equivalent of pleadings, where each party can set out its own position. Arbitrators generally require 'points of claim' and 'points of defence'.

If at oral hearing the parties fail to call evidence to prove a particular allegation that has been contested in the pleadings, the claim is likely to fail.

For example, in the 2005 Scottish case of *McTear v Imperial Tobacco Ltd*,[1] a widow sued a tobacco company following her husband's death from lung cancer. She claimed in her pleadings that he had smoked since 1964, with a preference for a particular brand of cigarette, and that the cancer had been caused by the cigarettes.

It may have been common knowledge for many decades that there was a causal link between cigarette smoking and lung cancer, but the plaintiff's legal team did not call sufficient expert evidence to prove it. In a very lengthy and detailed judgment, the court concluded that:

a) there was insufficient evidence that the tobacco company had ever accepted a causal connection between smoking and lung cancer;

b) the judge was not in a position to conclude there was such a link based on 'judicial knowledge' (i.e. a fact so notorious as to be indisputable);

c) insufficient epidemiological evidence had been given to establish such a causal connection; and

d) even if there had been sufficient epidemiological evidence, it would not have been sufficient to prove the individual causation in the case of the plaintiff's husband.

The claim therefore failed.

So, when the legal team is preparing the pleadings, it needs to consider not only what facts will be required to succeed in the claim, but whether it will be able to prove them. This will sometimes require detailed consultation with expert witnesses at an early stage of the case.

Particulars of pleadings

While the essential allegations may be pleaded in general terms, pleadings are often required to include 'particulars', which amount to more specific detail of the allegations. So, as well as setting out that the defendant, for example, breached the terms of a contract, the pleadings should set out some detail as to how the breach took place. This is where expert witnesses are likely to become involved in pleadings.

While the detail required may be straightforward in some cases, it will be complex in others. For example, to ground a case in professional negligence, it will be necessary to set out in some detail how the professional in question fell below the standard required. This will often require the legal team to take the report obtained from an expert and set out in the pleadings the detail contained in the report.

Where such 'particulars' are not included in the original pleadings the parties may claim that they do not have sufficient detail to prepare for the case. Generally, they are entitled to seek 'further and better particulars' by way of a notice. If the other party does not provide the information sought, an order may be sought from the court to compel the reply. It may be necessary to consult with the expert witnesses in order to prepare replies to such a notice.

As the case develops, further information is likely to be obtained in relation to certain issues. The compensation required will often not have been established in final detail at the time the original pleadings are issued, so the parties will need to update the particulars before the matter is heard. To prepare such updated particulars may also require updated expert reports, or consultation with experts, depending on the issues involved.

In some complex cases, there can be extensive wrangling concerning the matters to be pleaded in particulars requiring applications to the court. In general, the parties are entitled to such information from the other side as is necessary for them to prepare their case, but without seeking the minute detail of every allegation made.

Affidavits

An affidavit is a sworn statement of fact. While there may be a number of uses of affidavits, in litigation they are generally used to ground an application to a court where no oral evidence is required.

Because an affidavit is a sworn document, it is enforced in the same manner as if the deponent (the party swearing the affidavit) had given oral evidence from the witness box. A deponent who knowingly misleads the court may face a charge of perjury.

As with pleadings, because the facts need to underpin a legal application the affidavit is generally drafted by the legal team, but it is often sworn by a party or one of the witnesses, having given instructions.

Affidavits are commonly used in three types of hearing:

(i) **Procedural hearings:** Where, for example, a party is seeking to compel replies to a notice for particulars, or seeking discovery of documents, the application is grounded on (supported by) an affidavit. Often, the affidavit will simply set out the exchange of correspondence between the parties upon which the applicant is relying in seeking the order. Occasionally, it will be necessary for an expert witness to swear an affidavit. Where the party is seeking to obtain discovery of a particular type of document, or seeking an order to inspect a particular object or property, an expert witness might be asked to swear an affidavit explaining why this is needed. Alternatively, the affidavit might 'exhibit' a report or correspondence from the expert.

(ii) **Applications for injunctions** (or other interim or interlocutory orders): An injunction is generally an order to restrain a party from doing a particular thing, such as demolishing a building or selling a piece of property. When these are granted on an 'interim' or 'interlocutory' basis, the injunction is temporary, pending the final hearing of the case. Because such order may be granted on an urgent application, the grounding affidavits may be put together in a hurry. Experts may be required to swear affidavits in relation to certain factual information where injunctions are sought.

(iii) **Hearings where the facts are not thought to be controversial**: There are many types of court application that do not require oral evidence to be called. The factual information is put before the court on affidavit and the legal team makes submissions to the court based on the sworn information.

Where experts are asked to swear affidavits they should first ensure that they understand why the affidavit is required. They should also ensure that they can stand over any factual assertion made in the affidavit. As the affidavit is normally drafted by the legal team but sworn by the witness, it is possible for errors to creep in.

Once the affidavit has been sworn it becomes one of the documents in the case. The expert who has sworn it may be cross-examined as to its contents. If an uncorrected error has been included in an affidavit as sworn, this may be hard to explain at a later stage.

While affidavits were traditionally 'sworn' documents, meaning that the deponent was required to hold a religious book when making the oath, in more recent times many countries have adopted alternative practices. Recognising the decline of organised religion and the growth of multiculturalism, courts will often now accept a declaration or a 'statement of truth' instead. Statements of truth may have the same legal effect as a sworn affidavit in some countries, in that a witness can be prosecuted for knowingly misleading the court in such a document. Expert witnesses should ensure that they understand the legal effect of any such oath, declaration or statement of truth before they put their names to them.

'Scott Schedules'

> The Scott Schedule should be a detailed map to the claims asserted and defences raised, on an issue-by-issue basis, among all the parties. This map then becomes the outline for the evidence at trial and for the court's judgment itself.[2] (*Urbacon Building Groups Corp v Guelph (City)*, Superior Court of Justice, Ontario)

Often there will be a significant lapse of time between the original pleadings and the final hearing of the case. During that time, particulars may have been updated, discovery exchanged and expert reports prepared and submitted. The areas of dispute may have evolved from the time the case originally issued.

Rather than open the case to the court on the basis of the original pleadings, the parties may be required to prepare a document known as a 'Scott Schedule'.

Many lawyers are not familiar with Scott Schedules. In Henry Cecil's novel *Brothers in Law* (1955), the hero, Roger Thursby, is asked by the Official Referee if there is a Scott Schedule in a case for which he is completely unprepared. Roger has no idea what the judge is talking about:

> Roger suddenly had an urge to say: 'No, Your Honour, but I think there's an Irish stew.' That would be the end of his career at the Bar. Short and inglorious. But over.

In fact, 'Scott Schedules' were developed by George Alexander Scott (1862–1933), who was appointed Official Referee of the Supreme Court of Judicature in 1920. (The Official Referee's court in 1972 became the 'Technology and Construction Court' of the High Court of England and Wales.) Although Scott's life and career do not seem to have merited much note, an indication to his structured approach may be given by the fact that, prior to his appointment, he wrote some articles on the duties of auditors for the *Incorporated Accountant's Journal*.

The purpose of the Scott Schedule is that each party sets out, point by point, the case being made, and the other party addresses each point. Thus the court is able to see clearly on each point where the dispute lies.

In their simplest form, Scott Schedules are set out as a spreadsheet and contain seven headings:

- number of item;
- alleged defect (description in words);
- plaintiff's comments;
- plaintiff's cost estimate (in figures);
- defendant's response to defect (summary of reply);
- defendant's cost estimate (if appropriate); and
- comments of judge or arbitrator.

More detailed Scott Schedules might include columns referencing particular documents or witness statements.

Guidance for the preparation of Scott Schedules is given in the Civil Procedure Rules of the courts of England and Wales. They are widely used in arbitration, particularly of construction disputes. Provision is made for Scott Schedules in Australia for building and technical disputes.[3]

They are commonly used in Canada, where they were well-described in 2009 by Justice Corbett in the above-cited case of *Urbacon Building Groups Corp. v Guelph (City)*:

> In a large construction project such as this, Scott Schedules are generally organized in the following fashion. First, the parties set out their positions on what the contracts say (identifying the parties in privity, the contract price(s), and their respective positions on the extent to which the contract has been performed) and the contract accounting. Second, the parties set out their positions on "extras" to the contract, that is, work that was performed outside the scope of the contract, and the amounts claimed and/or paid in respect to such work. Third, the parties set out their positions in respect to alleged "deficiencies" in the work performed (these are defects in work actually performed, rather than work that has not yet been performed), including the alleged costs to remedy these deficiencies. Fourth, the parties set out their positions respecting the cost to complete the contract work. Fifth, the parties set out their positions respecting ancillary claims (such as damages for delay, alleged set-off claims arising from matters other than

the construction of the project at issue, and anything else that is alleged to affect the quantum claimed). Finally, a comprehensive Scott Schedule may also include a chart of the parties 'positions respecting technical issues such as the formal validity and timeliness of liens.

Although they were developed for construction cases, the courts of England and Wales also provide for the use of Scott Schedules in family law cases, specifically where domestic abuse of children is alleged. As part of its case management procedure in such cases, the court should consider:

> whether the key facts in dispute can be contained in a schedule or a table (known as a Scott Schedule) which sets out what the applicant complains of or alleges, what the respondent says in relation to each individual allegation or complaint; the allegations in the schedule should be focused on the factual issues to be tried; and if so, whether it is practicable for this schedule to be completed at the first hearing, with the assistance of the judge.[4]

They may also be directed in personal injury cases, such as the 2011 English case of *Locke v Stuart*,[5] a case arising from a road traffic accident. The judge complained about the quantity of documentary material put before the court. He commented:

> It should be possible to prepare a document, based on the documentation including the witness statement … and the 3 lever arch files of documents, together with the further 3 lever arch files of Facebook searches which accurately and fairly summarises their relevant contents so far as the primary facts are concerned. It can identify, in the manner of a Scott Schedule, which primary facts are in dispute so that the necessary material, and only the necessary material, can be adduced to deal with that. It may further also identify which inferences are agreed and which are not.

There is also precedent for the use of Scott Schedules in employment disputes before quasi-judicial bodies.[6]

Where a Scott Schedule is directed, it will require work by both legal teams and – in the appropriate sections – by the expert witnesses. Essentially, it requires them to address each point in the case, to set out for the court whether there is a dispute on that point, and to summarise what the dispute is.

The preparation of a Scott Schedule is of necessity time-consuming, but in complex cases it is likely to be a more cost-effective way of narrowing down the issues than allowing the matter to go before the court in reliance on the original pleadings.

Where expert witnesses are required to prepare Scott Schedules they can expect a number of drafts to be exchanged with the legal team before they are ready to submit to the other side or to the court.

The advantage of a Scott Schedule was outlined by Mr Justice Noonan in the 2016 Irish case of *WL Construction Ltd v Chawke*:[7]

> The efficacy of a Scott Schedule is of course entirely dependent on the parties setting out their stalls in a frank and forthright manner in it. The schedule is intended to give a summary of what the plaintiff's claim is and the defendant's response to it. Importantly also, the schedule contains a list of items agreed between the parties. Obviously the identification of agreement on items is of great assistance to the court being an indication that no adjudication is required on that particular item. It seems to me that once an item is agreed on a Scott Schedule, that is an end of the matter save perhaps in exceptional circumstances such as for example manifest mistake or non est factum. It has however, to all intents and purposes the same characteristic as the compromise of an individual claim in relation to the item agreed.

In advance of trial, as courts seek to narrow down issues by means of case management, exchange of expert reports and meetings between experts, it is likely that more use of Scott Schedules would result in a considerable saving of court time. A well-prepared Scott Schedule is a focused agenda for the parties and the court to follow at the hearing of the action.

Not only is the preparation of a Scott Schedule valuable for the court, it can be a useful exercise for the client and legal team to assess the strengths and weaknesses of every aspect of their case. An expert who understands the purpose of the schedule and takes time to prepare it properly would be a valuable asset.

Conclusion

Whenever an expert is asked to assist in the drafting of any document it is important to understand what the purpose of the document is. In general, experts should ensure that if they are involved the preparation of any document, the factual information put before the court is correct. This is especially true where experts are required to put their own names to documents. Where the document includes an oath, declaration or statement of truth, experts should ensure that they understand the legal implications.

Once all the documents are completed in the required manner, it will be necessary to prepare for the oral hearing of the case itself. This will be discussed in the next chapter.

Notes

1.   [2005] ScotCS CSOH_69(3) (31 May 2005).
2.   *Urbacon Building Groups Corp. v Guelph (City)* 2009 CanLII 72065 (ON SC).
3.   Australian Capital Territory, Court Procedures Rules 2006, Reg 431.
4.   Practice Direction 12J.
5.   [2011] EWHC 399 (QB) (25 February 2011).
6.   *British Transport Police Authority v Hill* UKEAT/0251/15/BA.
7.   [2016] IEHC 539.

Chapter 12

Oral Evidence at Hearing

Oral evidence is the process by which a trier of fact (a judge, jury or arbitrator) decides which of the factual allegations made by the parties and witnesses are more likely to be true.

In some cases, the main witnesses will give accounts that are completely contradictory, such that it must be concluded that one side is lying to the court. Sometimes this can be resolved by reference to concrete factual evidence (eg, photographs or documents) that are more consistent with one account than the other.

In other cases, there are subtler factual differences between the parties, and the trier of fact has to determine them based on the credibility of each witness, having observed them in the witness box.

Oral evidence by each witness is generally divided into two parts: examination-in-chief and cross-examination. Essentially, examination-in-chief is the opportunity for witnesses to give their own account. Cross-examination is the opportunity for the opposing side to test that account, by asking searching questions and putting to the witness any alternative propositions.

When it comes to the testimony of professional witnesses the matters to be resolved are likely to be different. Instead of determining which witness is telling the truth, or has a more reliable memory of events, the decision maker will need to address more technical issues. In recent years, many jurisdictions have considered that the traditional method of adducing evidence is not appropriate to professional witnesses, and have introduced a technique known as 'concurrent evidence', or 'hot-tubbing'.

In this chapter, the traditional methods of giving evidence are discussed first, followed by a discussion of 'concurrent evidence', and remote hearings.

Evidence-in-chief ('examination-in-chief', or 'direct evidence')

The purpose of evidence-in-chief is for witnesses to give their account of what took place in their own words.

The witness is questioned by one of the legal team on their own 'side', and there are rules to prevent them being prompted to give a particular answer. In general, only 'non-leading' questions are allowed, which means questions starting with: 'who', 'what', 'where', 'why', 'when', or 'how'. Witnesses may be asked to explain a portion of their testimony.

At times it can be difficult for the counsel to elicit from the witness the particular answer required. Where there is a particular fact that the legal team want the judge or jury to hear, it can be difficult to get the witness to give that answer without resorting to an impermissible 'leading question'.

As well as giving their own narrative account of what took place, the witnesses may be asked questions in anticipation of cross-examination. If the legal team is anticipating a particular line of questioning, it is often safest to deal with the issues in the evidence-in-chief, so that the cross-examination is less effective.

In some countries, where witness statements are exchanged between the parties in civil hearings, examination-in-chief is considered unnecessary and the parties proceed straight to cross-examination of the witness. This, of course, presupposes that the trier of fact will have properly read the witness statements prior to the cross-examination.

In the case of expert witnesses, where reports will normally have been exchanged between the parties, the evidence-in-chief should strongly resemble the material put forward in the reports. Issues may have arisen in pre-trial consultation that need to be elaborated upon, but there should be few surprises in the testimony given by experts in their evidence-in-chief.

Cross-examination generally

Cross-examination is where the other parties have an opportunity to question the witness in relation to matters relevant to the case. In general, cross-examiners seek to ask questions for the following purposes:

- to elicit or emphasise facts that are supportive of their own case;
- to establish facts damaging to the other party's case;
- to discredit the witness by showing that he or she is unreliable or actually dishonest.

In cross-examination, 'leading questions'(ie questions that seek to establish a particular answer) are not only allowed, but are the norm. The most effective cross-examination tends to be focused, establishing one fact at a time by means of leading questions eliciting 'yes' or 'no' answers, building up a picture that supports the cross-examiner's case.

If witnesses have given evidence that is not damaging to the other side's case, it is often more prudent not to cross-examine them. There is always a danger that they may give further evidence that will be damaging. Sometimes the parties themselves can find this frustrating, feeling that their lawyers should attack all of the other side's witnesses without realising the damage that can be done by unnecessary cross-examination.

Cross-examination does not have to be combative. If a witness for the other party gives frank factual evidence that is neutral in its effect, questions can be asked on cross-examination that simply elicit other, useful, factual information.

However, where a witness gives information that needs to be

contradicted or undermined, the cross-examiner needs to decide whether to take a combative approach.

Harry Ognall (a well-known Queens Counsel, and later High Court judge) commenting in his memoirs, mentioned the cross-examination in the Yorkshire Ripper case:

> As a very young man at the bar, I remember being led by a distinguished QC who once said to me of the art of cross-examination 'If you can't poison the atmosphere in the first ten minutes, then sit down'. Mindful of this, I spent literally hours of my preparation on what should be my first question of [a psychiatrist].[1]

Other cross-examiners prefer to adopt a friendly attitude for most of the cross-examination, building up a factual picture, lulling the witness into a false sense of security, and leaving any damaging questions to the very end.

Cross-examining an expert witness

Where professionals are giving evidence they may reasonably expect that the cross-examiner will have read through their reports line-by-line, seeking inconsistencies or omissions that may undermine their conclusions. In cases where substantial amounts of money are at stake, the legal team for the opposing party may have given considerable resources to investigating the other side's experts, including their qualifications, professional literature they have written, or other cases they have worked on.

The following issues are likely to be raised in cross-examination:

i. Facts that support the cross-examiner's own case: There may be some issues addressed in the expert's report that are more favourable to the opposing party than their own expert's report. The expert is likely to be asked to confirm these.

ii. Inconsistencies or omissions in the report: If the expert report includes internal inconsistencies or omissions, these will be highlighted.

iii. Inconsistencies between the report and the oral evidence: If the professional gives oral evidence that deviates from the material in the reports, it is probable that this will be highlighted.

iv. Any deficiencies in the professional's investigation: If it can be shown that the professional deviated from proper procedure during any investigation, this is likely to be highlighted. Generally, this is only likely to be successful if it can be shown that it materially affected the quality of the investigation, or amounted to such a significant omission as to raise a doubt that should be resolved in favour of the cross-examiner's client.

v. Inconsistencies between the expert's testimony and the testimony of other witnesses: If the professional has relied on accounts given by witnesses of fact, and their accounts differ in the witness box, this is likely to undermine the professional's conclusions. It may be that the witnesses have simply changed their testimony, which is out of the control of the professional. It could, however, raise doubts as to whether the professional took a reliable note of the account during the investigations.

vi. The specialist knowledge relied upon: It is generally risky for an advocate to cross-examine a professional on their own subject matter. In general, the professional should know substantially more about the subject than even the most diligent lawyer. Nonetheless, it is sometimes necessary to confront an expert witness on the relevant specialist knowledge. In general, a lawyer will only do this if it is possible to demonstrate that the expert witness is manifestly wrong, or has chosen to present the expertise in a manner that is clearly designed to assist the experts' own client.

vii. Other writings of the expert (or the expert's own colleagues): Where an expert has published material on the subject matter relevant to the case, it may be a fertile ground for a cross-examiner to show that the position was more nuanced than the expert has suggested in the witness box. Where colleagues of the expert have written on the subject, the expert may be reluctant to publicly contradict them.[2]

viii. The expert's qualifications: The other party is entitled to ask questions as to the qualifications of a person purporting to be an expert in a subject. Where the qualifications have been exaggerated, it is reasonable to expect that this will be relied upon to cast doubt on the reliability of the expert. Where one expert has more experience than another, the cross-examiner may seek to highlight this. Of course, a decision maker should be slow to prefer one expert's testimony to another simply because of a few years' difference of experience, and should attempt to resolve the matter by reference to the actual evidence. Nonetheless, some decision makers may be unduly impressed by such considerations.

ix. Other indications of bias: As expert witnesses are expected to be impartial, the cross-examiner is likely to seize upon any comments or omissions that suggest that the expert is attempting to favour their own client.[3]

Preparation by the expert witness to give oral evidence

Prior to giving evidence, expert witnesses should be thoroughly prepared to assist the court on the issue at hand. This means that they should review the primary materials, their own report and the reports of the other expert witnesses.

The expert should bear in mind that the cross-examiner is likely to have read through all the materials forensically, looking for inconsistencies and omissions, so at least be in a position to answer the questions at a factual level. Although the instructing legal team cannot suggest to the expert that a particular answer should be given, the areas of cross-examination are likely to have been discussed in consultation, and the expert should be in a position to assist the decision maker on those points.

Giving evidence

A few pointers may usefully be given to a prospective witness:

i. The witness should speak slowly and clearly: Although the answers are primarily for the judge or jury, it is important that everybody in the courtroom hears them clearly.

ii. Answers should be addressed to the decision maker: It is common for a cross-examiner to try to draw a witness into an argument, or to use technical language with which the judge or jury may not be familiar. The witness should always remember that the answers are for the benefit of the decision makers, and address them accordingly. This means, for example, that, if a question has been asked using complex technical language, the witness should ensure that the decision maker understands the language when giving the answer.

The American writer Janet Malcolm was sued for libel in the 1990s in San Francisco, arising from an article in the *New Yorker*. Following a disastrous cross-examination in the first trial by a lawyer called Charles Morgan, there was a jury disagreement on the award of damages, which meant that there was a second trial. Deciding to take no chances, Ms Malcolm attended a public speaking coach named Sam Chwat. (Such coaching is permitted in the US.) As recounted by Ms Malcolm in a later article, Sam Chwat advised her on who to address, as well as how to address them:

> "A trial jury is like an audience at a play that wants to be entertained. Witnesses, like stage actors, have to play to that audience if their performances are to be convincing. At the first trial I had been scarcely aware of the jury. When Morgan questioned me, I responded to him alone. Sam Chwat immediately corrected my misconception of whom to address: the jury, only the jury. As Morgan had been using me to communicate to the jury, I would need to learn how to use him to do the same."[4]

iii. A witness is entitled to consider the answer to a question: A question may be framed in such a way that a simple 'yes' or 'no' answer seems to be required, when the true answer may be more complicated. The witness should not feel rushed into an answer if time is needed to consider it.

iv. A witness is entitled to understand the question: If a witness is asked a question of a complex or hypothetical nature, the witness should not feel obliged to answer it without explanation.

v. A witness is normally entitled to elaborate on an answer to a question: One of the purposes of cross-examination is to put one party's side of the case to the witnesses for the other party, to give them the opportunity to explain or contradict it. However, cross-examiners tend to put their client's case in such a manner as to require a straightforward 'yes' or 'no' answer. If the witness feels that a more nuanced answer is required, the opportunity should be taken to give that answer. The cross-examiner will generally try to confine the witness to simple answers, and it may take some assertiveness to give a more elaborate one. However, the witness should try to keep any such elaboration to a minimum, so as not to confuse the decision maker.

vi. Giving evidence is not a memory test: If the witness cannot remember the answer, but will be able to assist the court by referring to the report or other materials, they may ask to refresh their memory by consulting them. This is normally permissible. But if the witness is constantly referring to the report for factual matters they should already know this is less likely to impress the decision maker.

vii. A witness should not guess the answer to a question: Because of the scrutiny of being in the witness box, witnesses are often embarrassed to admit that they do not know the answer to a question. This is a particular risk for expert witnesses who may feel professionally embarrassed to tell the court they do not know the answer. But if the alternative is to hazard a guess, or to get into a hypothetical discussion of what the answer might be, it is best to be frank with the court as to whether the witness is in a position to answer it.

viii. A witness should avoid getting into an argument with a cross-examiner: Sometimes, cross-examiners will try to goad witnesses into losing their temper or becoming involved in a heated discussion on matters tangential to the case. The purpose of oral examination is for the decision maker to establish the facts of the case. When an argument ensues, the decision maker is likely to become disengaged or unimpressed by the witness. The witness should resist any loss of temper and ensure that the answers are directed to the judge or jury in a manner that they understand.

ix. A witness should avoid attempts at humour: In most cases, the parties have quite a lot at stake, so any attempts at humour may be construed as not taking the case seriously enough. Sometimes, a cross-examiner will try to discredit the witness using humour, and this can be successful. Experienced advocates can be extremely funny at times. It is rare that witnesses will beat them at their own game, unless they are very experienced and confident public speakers. It is safest to stay focused on the subject matter, and not attempt to engage in a war of wits.

William L Prosser, former Dean of the College of Law at University College, Berkeley in California, had this to say about judges who tried to be funny, and the same point might be made about witnesses:

> The bench is not an appropriate place for unseemly levity. The litigant has vital interests at stake. His entire future, or even his life, may be trembling in the balance, and the robed buffoon who makes merry at his expense should be choked with his own wig.[5]

x. A witness should err on the side of formality: To be a persuasive witness, it is not necessary to be unduly eminent. Often, a judge or jury will be more engaged by a witness with a friendly and helpful demeanour, who answers questions in a clear and plain-speaking manner. But is inadvisable to slip into informality. A good professional witness will find out the appropriate way of addressing the decision maker (whether 'My Lord', 'Your Honour', 'Judge', 'Your Worship', 'Sir', 'Madam', 'Chairperson' or, in the case of a jury 'Ladies and Gentlemen') and examining lawyers. Even in arbitrations and mediations, which are often intended to be more informal settings, expert witnesses would be well-advised to retain a professional manner.

Concurrent evidence (or 'hot-tubbing')

> The two expert witnesses gave concurrent evidence. This exercise is becoming more frequent in the Commercial Court. The experts gave evidence together. Each outlined their position and commented on the

position of the other. I asked questions of each and in effect chaired a discussion of the issues. Counsel then asked questions of the experts. The receiving of the expert evidence in this manner expedites the process and serves to focus on the differences. The differences tend to be discussed by both experts at the same stage of the process rather than each expert holding the floor for the duration of their evidence before the other expert does the same. This approach is beneficial to an understanding of the differences. Expert witnesses would benefit from training in the giving of their evidence concurrently.[6] (*Aurora Leasing Ltd v Colliers International*, High Court of Northern Ireland)

The experts met and produced a joint statement summarising their views and the points of difference. In court their oral evidence was conducted as a concurrent evidence session or "hot tub". This involved taking series of topics which were the major points in issue. Each witness had the opportunity to express a view about the topic and counsel and the parties had a chance to ask questions on that topic (and going to expertise generally). I also was able to ask question to clarify matters. For this sort of evidence it was a very effective way of proceeding. From the point of view of the judge, the issues were dealt with logically and both expert's views expressed clearly. Common ground emerged on points of detail as well as a clear illumination of what the disagreement was. As best I can tell the whole exercise took up less time than sequential cross-examination would have.[7] (*Sudicka v Morgan*, High Court of England and Wales)

The process of giving 'concurrent evidence' is different from the standard approach of giving evidence-in-chief followed by cross-examination. The relevant experts are sworn in at the same time and give their evidence together. The practice, known as 'hot-tubbing' was developed in Australia, but has been adopted in many jurisdictions and by many international commercial arbitrators.

Instead of a formal hearing, where each question from counsel is followed by an answer from the witness, concurrent evidence is more like a committee meeting, chaired by the judge, who is also the decision maker. The process may vary, as can be seen from the quotations above. In the 2013 Northern Irish case of *Aurora Leasing Ltd v Colliers International*, the judge and experts engaged in a discussion, followed by questioning from counsel. In the 2019 English case of *Sudicka v Morgan*, the questioning by counsel took precedence, followed by questioning from the judge.

Concurrent evidence may also allow for the experts to question each other as to their findings and conclusions.

Judges appear to like the 'hot-tubbing' approach, as it allows them to guide the discussion, and go to the heart of the issues to be decided.

From the point of view of the legal team, the more informal approach of 'hot-tubbing' can come with risks. The legal teams have less control, and it moves from an adversarial process to a more inquisitorial process. If the experts are entitled to volunteer information rather than give an answer to a specific question, there is more danger that a talkative expert will make an unguarded comment or an unfavourable admission. There is also more danger that an overbearing expert will dominate the discussion.

The legal teams still have a role to play in the 'hot-tubbing' process, and it is primarily their job to ask the necessary questions to ensure that their case is properly presented.

When professional witnesses are directed to give concurrent evidence, they should understand the nature of the process, and be aware of the potential disadvantages. If possible, they should avoid getting into lengthy hypothetical or academic discussions that might give rise to unguarded comments. They should be aware that their more central role in giving evidence may require them to present their report or conclusions without the prompting of questions from the legal team.

If experts are allowed to ask questions of the other experts during the process they should prepare the relevant questions in advance. It may be that the questions could be prepared with the assistance of the instructing legal team, but this is a matter that the legal team will need to give specific guidance on, depending on the rules of the relevant jurisdiction.

Remote hearings

With developments in technology, remote hearings have become a more practical reality in recent years. It is now possible for most people to use video-conferencing facilities, and the COVID-19 pandemic of 2020 has led to a more widespread use of such technology throughout the world.

In principle, it should be possible for witnesses to give evidence remotely. In practice, many lawyers are reluctant to agree to allow contentious witnesses to give evidence by video facility. There are certain drawbacks. If evidence is given from another country or state, it may be harder to administer an oath or enforce the perjury or contempt laws against a person outside the jurisdiction of the court. Legislation may be needed in some countries to address this.

Where people are giving evidence from their homes, they may be subject to day-to-day distraction from family members, pets or visitors in a manner that would not be the case in court.

More seriously, if a person is giving evidence by way of a laptop or tablet computer, it is not possible to see whether there are other persons in the room who might prompt an answer to a question. Some judges and arbitrators require people to turn the computer or camera around at the beginning of the session to show that the person is alone, but this will not necessarily protect against somebody entering the room during the process.

Even the most sophisticated video conference software often has a small time-delay, which can affect the flow of evidence. Similarly, because the computer camera is generally set above the screen, it is not generally possible for the witnesses, lawyers or judge to make eye contact with each other. Witnesses can minimise this problem by use of a separate camera, and consciously looking away from the screen towards that camera when answering any question.

Particular problems may arise when a cross-examiner seeks to break down a defensive witness. There is a drama that arises in court when witnesses try to conceal information but are pinned down by the questioning. Their body language tells the court much about their attitude. Although the same questions may be asked by video conference, the remote nature of the hearing makes it impersonal, and the effect of the cross-examination may be lessened.

If professional witnesses are asked to give evidence by video, they should do their best to ensure that they give a good impression. Thought should be given to the lighting of the room, and to the background. They should ensure that their video and microphone are working properly, and it may be advisable to carry out preliminary 'screen tests'. They should dress as they would for court, and — bearing in mind that their face may be shown on a large screen— give some thought to their appearance. They should ensure that there will be no interruptions while they give their evidence, and should be prepared for a request to turn the camera around to show that there are no other people present. It would be advisable to speak more slowly than usual to ensure that everybody involved in the hearing can hear what is being said.

Conclusion

Whatever the form of evidence, whether evidence-in-chief, cross-examination, 'hot-tubbing' or video link, expert witnesses should remember that the primary purpose of their evidence is to assist the decision maker to reach the truth on any contentious issues of fact. A conscientious expert witness should not be afraid of giving evidence.

Similar considerations arise in other hearings, as will be discussed in the next chapter.

Notes

1   Harry Ognall, *A Life of Crime: The Memoirs of a High Court Judge* (William Collins 2017).

2   For a discussion on this topic by a renowned cross-examiner, see 'The Role of the Expert Witness', a 1999 essay by Adrian Hardiman SC, later Mr Justice Hardiman of the Supreme Court of Ireland. The essay was republished in Tottenham et al, *A Guide to Expert Witness Evidence* (Bloomsbury Professional, 2019).

3   For another discussion of this topic, see 'Effective strategies for cross-examining an expert witness' by Thomas C O'Brien and David D O'Brien, in *Litigation* (American Bar Association Journal), Vol 44, No 1, Fall 2017.

4   'A Second Chance', by Janet Malcolm, *New York Review of Books*, 24 September 2020.

5   Prosser, *The Judicial Humorist* (Little Brown 1952).

6   *Aurora Leasing Ltd v Colliers International* [2013] NIQB B1 (High Court of Northern Ireland, Weatherup J, 5 August 2013).

7   *Sudicka v Morgan* [2019] EWHC 311 (Ch) (High Court of England and Wales, Mr Justice Birss, 27 February 2019).

Chapter 13

Alternative Dispute Resolution

Alternative dispute resolution (ADR) is a catch-all term that covers a range of private dispute resolution services. Many parties prefer not to air their disputes in court, whether because of the public nature of court hearings, or because of a perception that the courts may not have an understanding of the type of issues being litigated.

Because of the different types of alternative dispute resolution, expert witnesses should have some idea of what is expected of them before they agree to attend. This chapter outlines some of the more common types of ADR, and the role of the expert in each.

Arbitration

Arbitration is a private alternative to litigation where, instead of the case being heard by a publicly-appointed judge, it is heard by an arbitrator appointed by the parties (or by a process agreed to by the parties). Expert evidence is often central to arbitration, because of the types of dispute involved.

Arbitration clauses in contracts

The arbitration process generally arises from a clause in a contract between the parties. They agree that, if a dispute arises, it will be determined by arbitration instead of litigation. This is a common feature of certain types of contract, most notably construction contracts and international commercial contracts. Often, standard form contracts, such as agreements for the purchase of vehicles, or package holiday contracts, will include an arbitration clause.

In most countries, arbitration is so well established as a process it receives statutory support. If one party to a contract issues court proceedings, the other party can apply to the court for a 'stay' on the litigation to allow the matter to be resolved by arbitration. At the conclusion of the arbitration process, the arbitrator's decision – normally known as the 'award' – can be enforced using similar mechanisms to court orders.

The UNCITRAL 'Model Law'

Because of the benefits of arbitration in international commerce, the United Nations Commission on International Trade Law (UNCITRAL) in 1985 prepared a 'Model Law on International Commercial Arbitration' (which was amended in 2006). This was designed to harmonise the international approach to arbitration by encouraging each country to adopt the law into its domestic legal system.

The Model Law has been largely adopted by most English-speaking countries. In others, most notably England and Wales (where London was already a leading centre of international arbitration), the arbitration legislation incorporates some features of the Model Law.

Advantages of arbitration

At an international level, arbitration is popular among commercial litigants as it avoids court processes that may be cumbersome, both because of delays in the system and issues of law. The arbitrator is appointed by and paid by the parties, so there is generally more incentive to bring the matter to an efficient conclusion.[1]

Another advantage, from the point of the view of many parties, is that arbitration is normally heard in private. This means that matters of a sensitive commercial nature that may be discussed in the arbitration will not be reported in the press.

Arbitration also has more finality than litigation. While most litigants have a right of appeal where the trial judge has made an error of law, the parties to an arbitration normally agree that the decision of the arbitrator will be final. The award can only be set aside by a court on very limited grounds.

Because of the private nature of arbitration, and because of the lack of an appeal mechanism, there is limited case law on the conduct of arbitrations. The parties and the arbitrator may agree their own processes.

Expert witnesses at arbitration

From the point of view of witnesses (expert or otherwise), their role in arbitration is likely to be similar to their role in litigation. The conduct of the arbitration may seem more informal. The arbitrator and lawyers will normally not wear legal attire, and the arbitration may be conducted around a boardroom table rather than a courtroom-type setting.

Most countries provide that witnesses to arbitration can be required to swear an oath in a manner similar to litigation. This means that they could be prosecuted for perjury if they knowingly misled the arbitrator. In practice, such prosecutions are rare.

It may reasonably be said that expert witnesses appearing at arbitrations are under the same duties as those appearing in court. That is to say that, irrespective of the party who is paying their fee, they should assume that their primary duty is to assist the arbitrator in reaching the correct decision. They should investigate the facts relevant to the issue they are asked to advise upon, conduct such professional research as is necessary, and deliver a reasoned conclusion on the issue. They should co-operate with the arbitration process, in terms of the delivery of reports, answering questions, meeting other experts and giving evidence.

Because arbitration is a common method of resolving construction disputes, Scott Schedules are widely used, and experts should be prepared to spend the time to complete them in a succinct and helpful manner.

Because of the flexibility of the arbitration process, some arbitrators will engage in 'concurrent evidence' ('hot-tubbing'), whereby the experts from each side give evidence at the same time, to be questioned by the arbitrator, the legal teams and each other.

Expert 'teaming'

The flexibility of arbitration allows arbitrators to experiment with other methods of resolving issues. One suggested approach to expert evidence is that of 'expert teaming'. Instead of the parties appointing their own experts, or the arbitrator appointing a single expert, each party may propose a list of, say, five experts who are qualified to advise on the relevant issue. The parties may make observations on each other's list, and the arbitrator can then choose two experts to act as an 'expert team' to assist in determining the particular issue.[2]

Powers of enforcement

In the absence of specific directions in the Model Law (or national legislation), the arbitrator's powers to enforce the duties of experts are similar to those of the trial judge, that is to say:

    (a) to rule the evidence of the witness inadmissible;
    (b) to give less weight to the evidence, such that the party retaining that expert is more likely to lose the case (or the relevant issue); and
    (c) make rulings on costs to account for any waste of time incurred as the result of any misconduct by the expert.

Similarly, if a professional witness in an arbitration process acts negligently or in an unprofessional manner, the same considerations will apply to professional negligence actions or fitness to practice actions as might apply to court proceedings.

Court interventions

It is unusual for courts to intervene in arbitration proceedings. However, as discussed elsewhere in this book, the courts of England and Wales in 2020 intervened where a firm of experts acting for a party in one arbitration then accepted instructions from another party in a related arbitration.[3] The judge held that the experts' duty of loyalty to the original client prevented them from acting for another client.

In some types of arbitration, particularly in construction cases, it is likely that most of the evidence will be given by expert witnesses of various sorts. If an expert witness is in any doubt as to the requirements of a particular arbitration, specific guidance should be sought from the legal team. In general, however, the role will be similar to that of an expert in litigation.[4]

This cannot be said, however, of the other main type of alternative dispute resolution – mediation – which makes very different requirements of all the people involved.

Mediation

> **Frank Warren**: I fight for my corner, sometimes to my detriment, by the way; like the court case I had with Don King many years ago. He and I could have sat down and sorted that out. But, you know what, I didn't want to sit down because I was so aggrieved at what happened.
>
> **Interviewer**: And it cost you several million?
>
> **Frank Warren:** Yeah I took it to the limit, the whole limit. I fought it all the way and then we had to compromise. So I had to wipe my mouth, to do the deal, 'cos I had to live to fight another day.

(Frank Warren, boxing promoter, on *Desert Island Discs*, BBC Radio 4, 24 January 2010.)

At the conclusion of litigation or arbitration, the losing party will often, like Frank Warren in the quotation above, look back to the chances they might have had to resolve the dispute. Sometimes, even winning parties will realise that the litigation was so draining in terms of time, money and anxiety that they will also regret not having resolved it earlier.

For this reason, in recent years, parties and lawyers have looked to other processes to seek early resolution of disputes. The most common is mediation.

Mediation is a process whereby a neutral third party – the mediator – attempts to broker a deal between the litigants. The process is completely different from litigation or arbitration, and it has more similarities with the settlement negotiations with which lawyers are familiar.

The decision maker in mediation

From the point of view of an expert witness, the most important consideration in mediation is the fact that the mediator is not the decision maker. Although the mediator directs the process of the mediation, the decision makers are the parties themselves. If the parties do not both agree to a resolution of the dispute, the matter will proceed to arbitration or litigation.

Without prejudice and confidentiality

Mediation is invariably conducted on a 'without prejudice' basis. This means that anything that is stated in the mediation is privileged. If a party makes an admission, or changes position in the course of the mediation, this cannot be used against that party in court.

As well as being conducted 'without prejudice', mediation is generally confidential. The parties, lawyers and other participants are normally required to sign a confidentiality agreement, meaning that they will not disclose any of the matters discussed. Sensitive family law cases, or cases involving commercial contracts, would often be resolved by mediation. Any family secrets or trade secrets discussed should remain secret. A breach of such a confidentiality agreement would often be actionable in itself.

Matters in dispute

Unlike arbitration or litigation, the mediation process is not bound by the terms of the dispute. Judges will generally try to avoid introducing issues that are not directly relevant to the case before the court. Mediators, on the other hand, will often explore other issues between the parties to see if they can be used as 'trading chips' to make a resolution of the central dispute more palatable. In fact, some mediators believe that it is better for more issues to be on the table, as it makes it easier for one party to accept compromise on the central dispute if the other party has given ground on other issues.

Emotional issues

Related to this is the fact that mediators can give much greater emphasis to emotional issues. Judges and arbitrators are supposed to decide cases on the law and the facts, without letting feelings cloud their judgment. This can often leave the parties feeling bruised. There is a therapeutic element to giving evidence in the witness box, yet witnesses are supposed to limit their testimony to factual matters. When attending a mediation, the parties can explain to the mediator why they feel the way they do about the case, and the mediator can take this into account when attempting to find a resolution.

Other interested parties

The fact that the parties themselves are the decision makers gives rise to other difficulties. A dispute may have arisen between two individuals, but other interested parties may be present. If a brother and sister are in a dispute over the will of a parent, each may have a spouse who attends the mediation and may have strong views over how the family members have dealt with each other over the years. Similarly, disputes between neighbours will often involve more than one family member on each side, some of whom may be more conciliatory than others. If companies are in dispute over contractual issues, there may be a number of directors or employees present who have different views as to how the matter should be resolved. A skilled mediator will not only have to deal with the issues between the parties to the dispute, but will need to ensure that all of the interested parties on either side are heard. Otherwise, a mediated agreement may break down quickly.

The mediation process

In terms of the process, in a mediation between two parties the mediators normally use three rooms: one 'plenary' room, where the mediator can gather both sides for discussion; and two 'break-out' or 'caucus' rooms, where each side can meet with the mediator alone, or discuss matters amongst themselves.

Some mediators prefer to keep the discussion in the plenary room, exploring the issues with the parties together. Others prefer to engage in 'shuttle diplomacy', taking proposals from one party to the other until agreement is reached. Many mediations involve an element of both.

The role of the legal teams

Because the decision makers in the mediation are the parties themselves, the legal teams often have less active involvement in mediations than they do in litigation or arbitration, where they would be central to the presentation of the case to the decision maker, and ask almost all of the questions.

For the mediation to work, the mediator needs to engage directly with the parties by asking them questions about the dispute, although the lawyers may assist in explaining certain issues. It is when agreement is reached in principle between the parties that the lawyers become more involved, as the agreement will need to be drafted in such a manner that it satisfies both sides, and is legally binding.

The role of the expert witness in mediation

It is difficult to be prescriptive about the role of expert witnesses in mediation. Many mediators take the view that only the parties themselves should be present, and any other witnesses – expert or otherwise – would be an unnecessary distraction.

There are times, however, when it is necessary to involve experts, but the involvement will be different depending on the issue that the individual expert is advising upon.

As discussed elsewhere in this book, most civil disputes break down into issues of liability and remedy.

Expert witnesses on liability

Where expert witnesses are advising on issues of liability, it is difficult to see how they could normally assist the mediation process. Each party will generally need to reach its own view as to how likely they are to succeed in the case. This will involve taking advice from expert witnesses independently.

If the expert witnesses on liability are brought to the 'plenary' room in a mediation, and each has come to a different view, the best that they can do to assist the resolution of the case is to explain their view to the parties in a frank manner, and answer questions honestly. If the experts engage in a hostile discussion, each of them wedded to their own entrenched opinion, it may demonstrate to the parties the hurdles that will need to be crossed to win the case, but it is unlikely to assist resolution.

Expert witnesses on remedy

By contrast, if one party has suffered loss or damage, and there is a dispute as to what will be necessary to remedy it, there may be benefit to experts attending to discuss the most constructive and cost-effective solutions. For example, if building defects have come to light in a construction dispute, it will be necessary to establish the best way of fixing them, whether or not an agreement is reached. The architects, engineers or quantity surveyors may be able to assist in finding the best course of action.

Experts on standby

It is likely that, at the outset of a mediation, the mediator and parties will not know how the discussions will evolve. It would be expensive to ask experts to attend if it is not known whether they will be needed.

It is also likely in relation to a number of issues that the experts would not need to attend in person. Questions may arise that could be answered by a phone call.

The more cost-effective way of dealing with expert witnesses may be to ask them to be 'on standby', either to answer questions by telephone, or to attend the mediation at short notice. If this approach is taken, the experts should consider whether to charge a 'standby fee'.

Presence of experts in caucus rooms

Expert witnesses who attend mediation should remember that their role is to be impartial. Throughout the process of the dispute, including any mediation, their primary duty is to the judge or arbitrator who will decide the case if it is not resolved.

Because the expert is supposed to be impartial, and is not a member of the legal team, it is questionable whether they should be present during any 'caucus' discussions. Parties may discuss confidential matters amongst themselves, or with the mediator, that should not form part of the expert's considerations when writing a report or giving evidence. Moreover, the expert might develop an emotional connection to the party by being present during fraught discussions.

Experts should therefore consider excusing themselves if they are not strictly needed for any part of the discussion. If the mediator is aware that experts are likely to be present, it may be best to arrange a separate room for them, or to schedule their attendance only for a time when they are likely to be needed.

Collaborative law (or collaborative practice)

Collaborative law is a process developed mainly for family law disputes. Where spouses are separating, they engage a trained practitioner, who may be a legal practitioner or a financial professional. They then engage other professionals, such as child specialists or financial professionals, all of whom should be trained in the process, to assist the parties to resolve any issues.

The participants sign a 'court disqualification clause' that prevents the professionals from acting for the parties in any future litigation. This is designed to give them an incentive to find a resolution.

The collaborative family law process was developed in the 1990s by a family lawyer named Stu Webb in the US state of Minnesota. Since then, it has been adopted as a practice in many other countries.

Lord Kerr of Tonaghmore, a UK Supreme Court judge, was sufficiently impressed with the system to recommend in 2009 that it be extended to other practice areas, including commercial disputes.[5] To date, it seems mainly to be confined to family disputes, but in principle it should be transferrable to other types of action.

Professionals who wish to act in collaborative law cases should obtain the appropriate training, which is available in many countries.

Conciliation

The term 'conciliation' is sometimes used as synonymous with mediation. But there is a specific type of conciliation that has been adopted in some contracts – primarily construction contracts – which is a hybrid between mediation and arbitration.

The role of the conciliator in such disputes is to encourage resolution between the parties. If resolution is not reached, the conciliator then makes a recommendation. The parties then have a certain length of time to decide whether to accept the recommendation, or to proceed to arbitration or litigation before a different decision maker.

Because the conciliator has a decision-making role (albeit a non-binding one), it is more likely that expert witnesses will be needed to advise on the issues. If asked to attend a meeting during the course of conciliation, experts should treat the conciliator as they would a judge or arbitrator, and assist in resolving the issues in an impartial manner.

Adjudication

Adjudication is a 'fast track' type of dispute resolution, mainly used in construction contracts. Where a dispute has arisen between, say, two contractors involved in a building project, there is a danger that it will hold up the whole project. Therefore, adjudication has very tight time limits for the appointment of an adjudicator, the filing of submissions by the parties and the issuing of a decision by the adjudicator.

The decision remains binding until and unless it is overturned by an arbitrator or judge.

The process is informal, but it is normally open to the parties to furnish the adjudicator with expert evidence.

Expert determination

An alternative to an arbitration clause in a contract is a clause requiring a dispute to be referred to an independent expert. This may arise where a contract is of a specialist nature, and a dispute is to be referred to a particular type of expert.

It has been held that a clause requiring expert determination is not the same as an arbitration clause, in the sense that it does not come under arbitration legislation (whether the UNCITRAL Model Law or otherwise).[6] The jurisdiction of the expert is therefore governed by the contract itself.

Expert determination is designed to reach a speedy and final resolution of a dispute, and it is likely to be informal in nature. Whether expert witnesses would give evidence in such a process would depend on the wording of the relevant dispute resolution clause and the directions of the independent expert.

Online dispute resolution

The term 'online dispute resolution' (ODR) is used to cover a variety of methods of resolving disputes using computer technology.

Because of the massive amount of online commerce using international marketplaces such as Amazon and eBay, it has been necessary to develop mechanisms to resolve disputes between buyers and sellers who are often in different countries. Most of these involve an algorithm, and are not handled by a decision maker or require any expert evidence. The platform developed for eBay and PayPal is said to handle over 60 million disputes per year.

Algorithms have also been used to develop 'visual blind bidding' systems, allowing parties to make open and 'blind' bids to settle disputes. The most well-known of these systems are Smartsettle ONE and Smartsettle Infinity, developed by Canadian engineer Dr Ernest Thiessen.

From an expert witness's point of view, it is more likely that they will encounter ODR as arbitration, mediation or conciliation using video-conferencing technology. Where parties to a dispute are in different locations, such technology is more cost-efficient than requiring them to travel to a particular venue.

Since the social distancing requirements of the COVID-19 pandemic, mediation by video-conferencing has become much more common.

If expert witnesses are required to engage in dispute resolution using video-conferencing technology, the same considerations apply as in online court hearings (see Chapter 12). Experts should give some thought to the presentation: ensure they are properly and professionally dressed and presented; ensure that the lighting and backdrop is appropriate; make sure that the technology (internet connection, video camera and microphone) is working; and make sure that there are no disturbances by people or animals.

Conclusion

Where expert witnesses are asked to engage with any alternative dispute resolution process, they should ensure that they understand their role. In general, when appearing at an arbitration, they should treat it as they would a court hearing, and focus on assisting the arbitrator in reaching a correct decision. When appearing at a mediation, they should seek to facilitate resolution – where possible.

Notes

1   For a survey on the advantages and disadvantages of commercial arbitration, see the *2018 International Arbitration Survey: The Evolution of International Arbitration,* published by White & Case.

2   'Expert Teaming: Bridging the Divide between Party-Appointed Experts and Tribunal-Appointed Experts', by Dr Nils Schmidt-Ahrendts', [2012] 43 VUWLR (*Victoria University of Wellington Law Review*). This is sometimes known as the 'Sachs Protocol', arising from a paper by Dr Klaus Sachs at the 2010 ICCA Congress in Rio de Janeiro.

3   *A v B* [2020] EWHC 809 (TCC) (03 April 2020); see Chapter 2 of this book.

4   For a very thorough discussion of the role of expert witnesses in international arbitration, see 'Expert Witness: Role and independence', by Sebastiano Nessi, in *New Developments in International Commercial Arbitration* (Schulthess 2016) by Mueller et al (ed).

5   'Senior Judge says 'collaborative' approach can be extended', by Frances Gibb *The Times* (8 October 2009); 'Collaborative law a success for divorcing couples, says judge', by Catherine Baksi, *The Law Society Gazette*, 15 October 2009.

6   See the English case of *Barclays Bank Plc v Nylon Capital LLP* [2011] EWCA Civ 826 (18 July 2011); and the Irish case of *Dunnes Stores v McCann* [2020] IESC 1 (22 January 2020).

Chapter 14

Other Hearings or Inquiries

Introduction

As well as court processes and alternative dispute resolution, there are other hearings that may involve expert witnesses. Some of these – like quasi-judicial bodies and professional disciplinary hearings – will be quite similar to court proceedings in that they involve an adversarial dispute. Others, such as parliamentary committees, public inquiries or inquests are more inquisitorial and can ask about more wide-ranging issues.

Before agreeing to appear before any hearing, it would be advisable for the professional witness to make the following enquiries:

(a) Who will be the chairperson or decision maker?
(b) Who will be the parties or interested parties?
(c) What are the decisions to be made or the issues to be addressed? Will the hearing be adversarial or inquisitorial?
(d) What are the particular issues the expert is being asked to give testimony on?
(e) Will the testimony be on oath?
(f) Can the witness be compelled by law to attend the hearing?
(g) Who is likely to be asking questions?
(h) Are other experts likely to be giving evidence?
(i) Are reports to be prepared by experts in advance of the hearing?
(j) Will the expert be entitled to examine relevant documentation or other materials prior to preparing a report or giving testimony?
(k) Will the expert be entitled to request further information, if necessary, for the expert to give an informed view?
(l) Will the hearing be in public or in private? Will it be recorded, filmed or broadcast?
(m) Will the expert be appearing on behalf of any particular party or interest group?
(n) Will the expert's subject matter be limited to the subject at hand, or might there be more wide-ranging questions?
(o) Will the expert be entitled to refuse to answer questions if they

are on an issue that had not been flagged in advance?

(p) Will the expert be under any particular duties that are distinct from those in a court setting? (ie those outlined in Chapter 2 of this book.)

Quasi-judicial bodies

Most countries have statutory bodies that are set up to determine particular types of dispute or issue, such as employment disputes, landlord and tenant disputes, probation hearings, planning issues or tax appeals.

These often take place in private and are of a more informal nature than court hearings—often because they are designed to accommodate lay litigants (persons representing themselves who do not have any formal legal training).

The issues determined by such bodies are often of a straightforward nature that would not require expert evidence. However, if experts do appear it should be assumed that their primary duty is to the decision maker, and they are otherwise under similar obligations to assist the process as they would be for a court.

Professional disciplinary hearings

Most professions are subject to regulation from a professional body that has the power to discipline its members. This power is generally exercised through a body such as a 'fitness to practise committee' that can enquire into any allegations of misconduct. Expert evidence is often required from a similar professional to assist the body to reach a decision.

Purpose of disciplinary hearings

The purpose of such bodies is to protect the public from professionals who have fallen below the standard expected, as well as to protect the reputation of the profession itself. Where people hold themselves out to be, for example, architects, accountants, medical professionals or lawyers, it is expected that they will have received the appropriate training, apply it in a professional manner in their dealings with their clients, and behave honestly. If an allegation is made that they have not done so, the professional body should intervene to uphold the standards and integrity of the profession.

On the other hand, the professionals in question rely for their livelihood on their good standing within their professional body. Allegations made against them of professional misconduct should not be treated lightly. If the allegations are upheld by the professional body, the professionals in question may lose their income. If the allegations are not upheld, an incompetent or dishonest person may continue to practise, to the detriment of the community.

Such cases are prosecutions in the public interest, with the option of disciplining the defendant. They are not civil claims for compensation.

Disciplinary measures available

The range of measures available to such a body will be prescribed individually and are normally governed by statute, but they can include:

- a finding of 'poor professional practice';
- a recommendation that the professional undergo training in a particular area of concern;
- suspension of the professional from practice; or
- striking the professional from the membership of the organisation (or the 'roll' of practitioners).

Standard of proof–'beyond a reasonable doubt', 'balance of probabilities', or another standard?

Because of the balancing considerations, a question has often arisen as to the standard of proof to apply in such cases. To apply the criminal standard of 'beyond a reasonable doubt' may seem unduly onerous where a serious allegation has been made against a professional. But, if the civil standard of the 'balance of probabilities' is applied, a professional person could lose their livelihood in a case where the evidence was only marginally against them.

The Canadian courts have grappled with this issue in a number of cases, and it was considered in the 1985 case of *Jory v College of Physicians & Surgeons of B.C.*:[1]

> The standard of proof required in cases such as this is high. It is not the criminal standard of proof beyond a reasonable doubt. But it is something more than a bare balance of probabilities. The authorities establish that the case against a professional person in a disciplinary hearing must be proved by a fair and reasonable preponderance of credible evidence ... The evidence must be sufficiently cogent to make it safe to uphold the findings with all the consequences for the professional person's career and status in the community ...

So, in some countries or professions, the civil standard applies. In others, the criminal standard applies. In other still, there is a hybrid standard.

Burden of proof

Irrespective of which standard is relevant, the burden of proof will be on the prosecution side to adduce evidence to establish the misconduct of the professional in question. So the prosecution, as in a criminal case, must be required to adopt an even-handed approach, disclosing to the tribunal not only facts that are consistent with the guilt of the professional, but also facts consistent with innocence.

Obligations of expert witnesses at disciplinary tribunals

A similar obligation will normally apply to any expert witness. It may be assumed that a witness called by the prosecution (or any independent expert) should disclose any information that is consistent with the innocence of the professional. The tribunal should be in a position to make its decision based on the full facts of the case.

This includes information about the relevant specialist knowledge. If, for example, one professional textbook suggested that the conduct in question was unacceptable, but another one suggested that it might be appropriate, the prosecution expert should disclose both to the tribunal.

Witnesses at such hearings should be particularly conscious of potential conflicts of interest. Professionals in any field are likely to have encountered each other, or worked in similar institutions. If colleagues are called as witnesses as to fact, they should normally limit their testimony to factual issues, and not express an opinion as to the professional standard involved. At times, it can be difficult for professional witnesses of fact to avoid straying into an expression of opinion but the tribunal will have to give the appropriate weight to such expressions if there is a conflict of interest.

Parliamentary committees

Most parliaments in democratic countries have committees with a range of functions, and they generally have the power to question witnesses.

At their best, such committees hold the government to account in particular areas and help decide on what legislation to put in place. But they also provide an opportunity for publicity-seeking parliamentarians to grandstand, and place clips of their clever questioning on social media.

Some parliamentary hearings are notorious. In April 1994, the chief executives of the seven largest tobacco companies in the US testified before Congress. Each of them said, in sworn testimony, that they did not believed nicotine was addictive, relying on a particular definition of addictiveness that suited their purpose. This exposed them to ridicule, as the footage was broadcast internationally, and conflicted with public understanding of the addictiveness of cigarettes.

Nature of parliamentary committees

Parliamentary committees may be established on a permanent basis, to scrutinise the workings of a particular government department, or on an 'ad hoc' basis, to examine a specific issue. New legislation will normally be scrutinised by committees, which have the power to propose particular amendments. Sometimes they are established on a 'post-legislative' basis, to see whether the objectives of the legislation were achieved. Committees may have the power to scrutinise particular government appointments, and question them as to the suitability of their role.[2]

Powers to invite and compel witnesses

Such committees normally have the power to invite witnesses to appear and give evidence. Sometimes they have the power to compel the attendance of a witness by subpoena, although this is rarely invoked in most countries. Sometimes, committees established to discuss a particular topic will invite submissions from members of the public. Where a particular industry is likely to be affected by proposed legislation, it is likely that they will seek to make submissions that are based on expert testimony.

Evidence on oath

Evidence before such committees may be given on oath, with the result that a charge of perjury may arise if the witness knowingly gives misleading evidence. Even if the evidence is not given on oath, some countries provide that false evidence may result in a change of perjury.[3]

Contempt of parliament

As well as the risk of perjury, witnesses may fact a charge of 'contempt of parliament' if they do not co-operate with the requirements of such a committee. This offence exists in many countries, and broadly corresponds with the offence of 'contempt of court'. A witness may be charged with contempt of parliament for: refusing to take the oath; refusing to answer questions; wilfully disclosing confidential information; or obstructing the work of the committee. It would also be contempt of parliament for another person to interfere with the evidence of a witness.

Traditionally, contempt of parliament was declared by a resolution of the parliament itself. In 2018, the UK government was found to be in contempt of parliament by a vote of MPs, after failing to comply with a resolution requiring that legal advice be published concerning the departure of the UK from the European Union. In most countries, penalties for contempt of parliament are imposed by the courts.

Duties of expert witnesses before parliamentary committees

Where witnesses give evidence to parliamentary committees in a professional or specialist capacity, they should assume that their primary duty is to the members of the committee, to give them the benefit of their specialist knowledge in deciding on the course of action before them. It should be assumed that experts would disclose any connection with interested parties, such as industries likely to be affected by proposed legislation. It is, of course, reasonable for a professional working for a particular industry to highlight matters that might not otherwise have been contemplated by the committee, but this should not be done in a manner likely to mislead.

Parliamentary privilege

Statements made in evidence before parliamentary committees are normally subject to parliamentary privilege. This means that a statement made concerning a third party may not be the subject matter of defamation proceedings.

However, such proceedings are normally subject to the *sub judice* rule. This means, that, because of the public nature of such hearings, they should not discuss cases pending before the courts in case they prejudice their outcome.

Public or private hearings

While the questioning of witnesses before parliamentary committees is normally conducted in public, some countries provide that the witness can apply for a private hearing.[4]

Legal representation of witnesses

If experts have particular concerns about the likely questioning, some countries provide that they can apply to be accompanied by a legal representative. An application would normally need to be made in advance of the hearing. If acting in a purely expert capacity, it is difficult to see why this might be necessary. However, if professionals are also acting as representatives of a particular company, industry or interest group, and there is a danger of incrimination of themselves or others if certain questions are answered, it might be considered advisable to have a legal representative.

As a general rule, any experts asked to attend before a parliamentary committee would be wise to establish what procedures will be adopted, and what protections there are for witnesses.

Public inquiries (tribunals of inquiry)

Most common law countries have provisions for public inquiries, tribunals of inquiry or royal commissions. These are normally 'ad hoc' tribunals set up to investigate matters of public interest. They normally have public hearings and witnesses may give evidence and face cross-examination. They are often chaired by a judge or member of the legal profession. In the United Kingdom, the legislation providing for tribunals of inquiry was established in 1921, because parliamentary committees were considered to be inadequate to deal with certain issues. Royal commissions, which are held in many Commonwealth countries, tend to inquire into general topics, while public inquiries tend to address more specific events of public concern.

In the UK, such tribunals have included:

- the Scott Inquiry into the sale of arms to the Iraqi government;
- the Saville Inquiry into the shooting dead of several civilians by British soldiers in Northern Ireland on 'Bloody Sunday'; and
- the Leveson Inquiry into the conduct of the British tabloid press after a telephone hacking scandal.

In Canada, an inquiry was held in the 1980s concerning allegations that Nazi war criminals had settled in the country following the Second World War. In Ireland, a number of tribunals have been established over recent decades to investigate allegations of planning corruption, payments to politicians, certain practices of the beef export industry, and police (Garda) practices.

Ideally, such tribunals have clearly defined terms of reference and conclude with recommendations for changes in legislation or government practice. If they are not kept tightly within the terms of reference, however, it is possible for interested parties to introduce other tangential issues. The result is that tribunals can run for much longer than was originally expected and cost significantly more.

Experts giving testimony before such inquiries should understand that they are inquisitorial rather than adversarial. The chairperson has an investigative role, and is often assisted by a legal team as well as experts or assessors.

Expert evidence may also be advanced by the interested parties to the tribunal, subject to the ruling of the chairperson. If the practices in a particular industry were under scrutiny, it would be reasonable for relevant companies to put forward specialists to assist the chairperson to understand particular issues. These might include specialists employed by the industry or independent experts, depending on the issue. As with courtroom testimony, it would be reasonable for an employed expert to give evidence of a more factual nature concerning the question, and for an independent expert to give evidence that is more relevant to the views of the profession, but the distinction may not be clear. It would be a matter for the chairperson to determine whether the testimony of a particular expert would be of assistance.

Any experts asked to give evidence to a public inquiry should consider the terms of reference of the inquiry, and be clear as to the issue or issues they are asked to advise upon. Because such inquiries can sometimes investigate issues of a wide-ranging nature, there is a risk that questioning could stray into unanticipated areas.

Expert witnesses might in certain circumstances want to be accompanied by a legal advisor. If they are present in a professional capacity, but are representing a particular interested party (for example, an industry concerned with the subject matter of the inquiry), there may be a risk of findings adverse to that party. If there were a risk of incrimination of the company, it would need to be established whether they were entitled to refuse to answer a particular question.

Where findings of fact are made that include findings of a criminal nature, this can present particular problems. The findings will tarnish the names of those accused, and can normally be published without fear of defamation proceedings, but the result is that any future criminal proceedings may be prejudiced.

Unless directed otherwise, experts should assume that the same duties apply in a public inquiry as in a court (ie the duties outlined in Chapter 2).

At the conclusion of the inquiry, the chairperson usually submits a report to parliament in a manner similar to a parliamentary committee. This is, of necessity, non-binding, but would normally include findings of fact and recommendations for future practice. Sometimes, there is political will to implement the recommendations. Sometimes, after months – or years – of detailed investigation, the report is simply shelved.

Inquests

Like public inquiries, inquests differ from normal courts in that they are inquisitorial rather than adversarial. In England, inquests date back to Norman times. Traditionally, they involved a jury.

Inquests are established into a death when there is a public interest in inquiring into the circumstances. This may include where an unidentified body is found, or where the death is unexpected, unexplained or suspicious. Some countries make provision for mandatory inquests in certain circumstances, such as deaths in prison or police custody.

Inquests are normally heard by a coroner (so called, because the coroner traditionally represented the crown), and some countries still provide for juries to make determinations in some or all cases.

Usually, the determinations made by inquests are factual:

> (a) the identity of the deceased;
> (b) where the deceased died;
> (c) when the deceased died; and
> (d) how the deceased died.

It is not the primary purpose of the inquest to make findings of fault, but fault may often be implied by the final determination. The inquest will often investigate lines of inquiry that might lead to blame being attached to certain people or organisations. While findings of suicide or homicide may sometimes be made, verdicts will often include 'natural causes', 'accidental death' or 'death by misadventure' (which differs from accidental death in that it arises where the deceased is found to have undertaken activity that involved a certain risk, such as a dangerous sporting activity or taking illegal drugs).

Expert evidence would normally be given by pathologists at inquests, as well as other relevant parties, such as police investigators.

Although findings of fault may not be made at inquests, relevant parties are often entitled to legal representation for the purpose of asking questions. The family of the deceased would normally be entitled to attend and ask questions. If a person died in hospital in unexplained circumstances, the medical professionals might be legally represented. If the deceased died in the workplace, the employer might be represented. Questions could be asked to elicit information to be used in other forums, such as medical negligence proceedings or an action against an employer.

Because of the inquisitorial nature of inquests, a question may arise concerning the privilege attached to expert reports (ie whether the party who obtained the reports is obliged to disclose them). This arose in the 2020 Northern Irish case of *Re Ketcher*,[5] where the mothers of two deceased soldiers obtained their own expert psychiatric report for an inquest. Because of the inquisitorial nature of the inquest, the coroner took the view that the expert report was not privileged and should be disclosed. This decision was upheld on judicial review. The Northern Irish Court of Appeal acknowledged that aspects of the inquest process were inquisitorial, but acknowledged that certain types of deaths led to inquests that were adversarial in nature. If the 'dominant purpose' of the report was for the purpose of civil proceedings, it would be privileged. Because it had been prepared for an inquest, it was not privileged (although the court strongly questioned whether it was in the public interest to order disclosure of the report).

So, if an expert is asked to prepare a report for an inquest, it would be appropriate to ask if this is the dominant purpose of the report, or whether it is also intended for contemplated litigation.

Conclusion

The fundamental duties of expert witnesses are unlikely to change whatever forum in which they appear. Unless directed otherwise, they should assume that their role as experts requires them to provide specialist knowledge to the decision maker in an impartial manner. At all times, they will be under an obligation to tell the truth on any factual matters.

The reality is, however, that expert witnesses are less likely to be professionally embarrassed before such hearings if they have a good understanding of the processes, and the questions they are likely to be asked. While this chapter addresses the possible forums in broad terms, experts should make the appropriate enquiries before giving testimony at any inquiry.

Notes

1.   BCSC, Vancouver No A850601, 13 December 1985.
2.   'Select Committees: Powers and Functions' by Richard Kelly, Ch 7 of *Parliament and the Law* by Horne et al (ed) (2013).
3.   See, for example, section 1A of the United Kingdom's Perjury Act 1911 (as amended in 1975).
4.   See, for example, the Parliament of Australia's 'Procedures to be observed by Senate Committees for the protection of witnesses'.
5.   [2020] NICA 31 (03 June 2020).

Conclusion

Advocating for the Truth

Throughout this book, the point has been emphasised that expert or professional witnesses should never act as advocates for their clients. This does not mean that they have no advocacy role.

When dealing with any clients, professionals need to persuade and to inform. Some clients are quite compliant, and will accept any recommendation from their doctor, dentist, mechanic, builder or lawyer. It is sometimes necessary to pin them down to their own decisions, so that they are not disappointed with the final result. Other clients can be notoriously demanding, questioning everything, even after the professionals involved think that the issue is settled. The professionals need to ensure that the underlying facts are clear, and that the reasons for the advice are understood. With some clients, it is necessary to have deep reserves of patience and good humour.

When expert witnesses are retained in contentious litigation, it is akin dealing to with a range of clients, many of whom may seem very demanding indeed. The instructing party and legal team themselves will not always be easy. They may try to infer certain conclusions from their own experts' reports, and seek to present them in a certain way to the court. The experts may need to correct them, and ensure that the reports and their conclusions are properly understood.

When dealing with questions from the other parties and legal teams, the experts face a different type of challenge. Attempts are likely to be made to undermine the experts and their work, to suggest that established facts are incorrect, and to raise doubt where there is no reasonable doubt.

Finally, the experts have to deal with the decision makers. Unlike the parties and their legal teams, the decision makers—whether judges, juries, arbitrators, or coroners—should have no vested interest in the outcome. While this has the benefit that they should decide cases on an objective basis, the danger is that they may not always give cases the attention they deserve. Judges and arbitrators can find themselves hearing cases concerning subject matter they are not familiar with, and sometimes need to decide several complex and varied cases in the same week. Some jury members may find it difficult to follow complex cases. The challenge for the expert will be to make the evidence both understandable and interesting.

So, while expert witnesses should not advocate for their clients, they should advocate for the truth. They need to correct any misrepresentations of fact, whether accidental or intentional. They need to present their evidence in a manner that will engage their listeners. And they need to be able to stand over their honestly-held conclusions.

In much of this book, examples have been given of expert evidence that has not met the standard required. But we shall finish with an account of how an expert witness was able to stand over his evidence and silence his cross-examiners.

The late Professor Robert Daly was an Irish psychiatrist with experience of working with the US Air Force. In 1971, after the 'Troubles' had started in Northern Ireland, the UK government introduced internment without trial of person suspected of paramilitary involvement — almost all from the nationalist population. Some of these people were taken for special questioning, involving what were euphemistically described as "five techniques". These included: prolonged standing against a wall, 'spreadeagled' with arms and legs outstretched; hooding for long periods; sleep deprivation; deprivation of food and drink; and subjection to 'white noise'.

The Irish government brought a case against the British government in the European Court of Human Rights, alleging that these techniques amounted to torture. Evidence was given by Professor

Daly at the 1973 hearing in the European Commission of Human Rights, in what became known as the 'hooded men' case.

Michael Lillis, then a junior official in Ireland's Department of Foreign Affairs, was present at the hearing, and described it later in a letter to the *Irish Times* newspaper in 2020, in response to an obituary of Robert Daly:

> *"Prof Daly was being cross-examined by the UK attorney general and other prominent British silks in the hectoring traditions of the Old Bailey. The tone began to change when Prof Daly explained that as a young psychiatrist in the US he had consulted for some years for the US Air Force who were training American military personnel who might be captured in combat to resist sophisticated forms of torture, including the "five techniques" that the Irish government alleged amounted to torture.*
>
> *He explained how knowledge of these "techniques" had originated with the debriefing by US experts of the crew of the US Navy vessel USS Pueblo which had been captured by North Korea in January 1968.*
>
> *During 10 months the captain and crew were subjected to various forms of torture, including the "five techniques". Several suffered long-term psychological and physical damage.*
>
> *By now the hectoring had stopped and was replaced by an expectant silence from the commission members and the entire courtroom. Prof Daly produced irrefutable written evidence from US government sources of the transmission of the findings by the US medical and intelligence authorities on the impact on their victims of the North Korean techniques to their counterparts in the UK.*
>
> *He explained devastatingly how British medical and security experts had used these methods on the 14 "hooded men" knowing beforehand how damaging their effects could be, including possibly major damage to a victim's nervous system.*
>
> *The British attorney general and his team made no attempt to refute any of this."*

The Commission ruled that the "five techniques" amounted to torture.[1] The case was referred to the Court of Human Rights, which concluded in 1978 that they were 'inhuman and degrading', but did not amount to torture.[2] The question remains controversial at an international level. Several countries continue to use some of the 'five techniques' in questioning, although it should be noted that they have been prohibited by the UK government at home and abroad since the 1972 publication of the 'Parker Report' following a Commission of Inquiry.[3]

Nonetheless, the testimony of Professor Daly shows how a well-prepared expert can advocate for the truth in the face of hostile cross-examination.

Notes

1   Their report was published on 9 February 1976.
2   *Ireland v United Kingdom* (5310/71) [1978] ECHR 1.
3   For a summary of the conclusions of the Parker Report, see the *Irish Times*, 3 March 1972. For a detailed outline of the case and the ensuing investigations, see the High Court judgment in *Re McGuigan and McKenna* [2017] NIQB 96; and the subsequent appeal, [2019] NICA 46.

APPENDIX 1

Checklist for Accepting Instructions

CHECKLIST FOR PROPOSED EXPERT WITNESS PRIOR TO ACCEPTING INSTRUCTIONS

a. Name of client:

b. Name of instructing law firm:

c. Name of case (if proceedings issued):

d. Subject matter of case:

e. Issue(s) requiring expert determination:

f. What is the relevant legal test concerning the issue(s)?

g. Is the proposed expert witness appropriately qualified to advise on issue(s)?

h. Is there a personal connection between the proposed expert witness and one of the parties?

i. Is there a financial connection between the proposed expert witness and one of the parties?

j. Are there any other matters that should be disclosed to the client or legal team that might affect the weight to be given to the proposed expert witness's evidence?

k. What formal declaration does the court (or arbitrator) require from the expert witness concerning duties or conflicts of interest?

l. Have fees been agreed between the proposed expert witness and the client or legal team?

m. Does the fee agreement cover all work that is likely to arise in the course of the proceedings?

n. Does the fee agreement cover any other members of staff or contractors that may be required?

o. Do the fee arrangements need to be disclosed to the court or other parties (eg. if a success fee is involved)?

p. Does the proposed expert witness have an insurance policy that covers this type of work?

Appendix 2

Checklist for an Expert Report

a. Name of client:

b. Name of instructing law firm:

c. Name of case (if proceedings issued):

d. Subject matter of case:

e. Issue(s) requiring expert determination:

f. Relevant legal test(s) (if applicable):

g. Qualifications of expert (include CV as appendix if required):

h. Statement acknowledging duty to the court (in the form required):

i. Statement of truth (if required):

j. Disclosure of any personal, family or financial connections (in the form required by the court, if applicable):

k. Factual investigations carried out (whether on-site or documentary):

l. Materials assembled (photographs, sketches, graphs, measurements etc–include in appendices if required):

m. Documents consulted:

n. Factual conclusions reached:

o. Professional research carried out (textbooks, legislative standards, professional standards, industry standards, comparators etc–include in appendices if required):

p. Reasoned conclusions on the issue(s) requiring expert determination:

q. Consideration of any other opinions or explanations concerning the issue that have been or are likely to be put forward:

r. Has report been proofread for spelling, references, grammar and readability?

Appendix 3

Case Law on Duties of Expert Witnesses(*The Ikarian Reefer*, and *Anglo Group PLC v Winther Brown*)

In Chapter 2 of this book, the duties of expert witnesses are broken down and discussed. In many countries, however, the courts have relied on the list of duties set out in the 1993 English case of *National Justice Compania Naviera SA v Prudential Assurance Company Ltd*, generally known as '*The Ikarian Reefer*'.[1]

In the 2000 English case of *Anglo Group PLC v Winther Brown and Co Ltd*,[2] the duties were 'extended' in light of the changes in English civil procedure known as the 'Woolf Reforms'.

The relevant excerpts are set out below.

a) The Ikarian Reefer (1993)

Mr Justice Cresswell:

> "The duties and responsibilities of expert witnesses in civil cases include the following:
> 1. Expert evidence presented to the Court should be, and should be seen to be, the independent product of the expert uninfluenced as to form or content by the exigencies of litigation (*Whitehouse v. Jordan* [1981] 1 W.L.R. 246 at p. 256, per Lord Wilberforce).
> 2. An expert witness should provide independent assistance to the Court by way of objective unbiased opinion in relation to matters within his expertise (see *Polivitte Ltd. v. Commercial*

Union Assurance Co. Plc. [1987] 1 Lloyd's Rep. 379 at p. 386 per Mr. Justice Garland and *Re J* [1990] F.C.R. 193 per Mr. Justice Cazalet). An expert witness in the High Court should never assume the role of an advocate.

3. An expert witness should state the facts or assumption upon which his opinion is based. He should not omit to consider material facts which could detract from his concluded opinion (*Re J* sup.).

4. An expert witness should make it clear when a particular question or issue falls outside his expertise.

5. If an expert's opinion is not properly researched because he considers that insufficient data is available, then this must be stated with an indication that the opinion is no more than a provisional one (*Re J* sup.). In cases where an expert witness who has prepared a report could not assert that the report contained the truth, the whole truth and nothing but the truth without some qualification, that qualification should be stated in the report (*Derby & Co. Ltd. and Others v. Weldon and Others*, The Times, Nov. 9, 1990 per Lord Justice Staughton).

6. If, after exchange of reports, an expert witness changes his view on a material matter having read the other side's expert's report or for any other reason, such change of view should be communicated (through legal representatives) to the other side without delay and when appropriate to the Court.

7. Where expert evidence refers to photographs, plans, calculations, analyses, measurements, survey reports or other similar documents, these must be provided to the opposite party at the same time as the exchange of reports (see 15.5 of the Guide to Commercial Court Practice)."

b) *Anglo Group PLC v. Winther Brown* (2000)

Mr Justice Toulmin:

"1. An expert witness should at all stages in the procedure, on the basis of the evidence as he understands it, provide independent assistance to the court and the parties by way of objective unbiased opinion in relation to matters within his expertise. This applies as much to the initial meetings of experts as to evidence at trial. An expert witness should never assume the role of an advocate .

2. The expert's evidence should normally be confined to technical matters on which the court will be assisted by receiving an explanation, or to evidence of common professional practice. The expert witness should not give evidence or opinions as to what the expert himself would have

done in similar circumstances or otherwise seek to usurp the role of the judge.

3. He should co-operate with the expert of the other party or parties in attempting to narrow the technical issues in dispute at the earliest possible stage of the procedure and to eliminate or place in context any peripheral issues. He should co-operate with the other expert(s) in attending without prejudice meetings as necessary and in seeking to find areas of agreement and to define precisely arrears of disagreement to be set out in the joint statement of experts ordered by the court.

4. The expert evidence presented to the court should be, and be seen to be, the independent product of the expert uninfluenced as to form or content by the exigencies of the litigation.

5. An expert witness should state the facts or assumptions upon which his opinion is based. He should not omit to consider material facts which could detract from his concluded opinion.

6. An expert witness should make it clear when a particular question or issue falls outside his expertise.

7. Where an expert is of the opinion that his conclusions are based on inadequate factual information he should say so explicitly.

8. An expert should be ready to reconsider his opinion, and if appropriate, to change his mind when he has received new information or has considered the opinion of the other expert . He should do so at the earliest opportunity."

Notes

1   [1993] 2 Lloyd's Rep 68.
2   [2000] EWHC Technology 127.

Index